The Science Behind the Benefits of Religion

How God Works

David DeSteno

Simon & Schuster
New York   London   Toronto   Sydney   New Delhi

Simon & Schuster
1230 Avenue of the Americas
New York, NY 10020

First Simon & Schuster hardcover edition September 2021

SIMON & SCHUSTER and colophon are registered trademarks of Simon & Schuster, Inc.

For information about special discounts for bulk purchases, please contact Simon & Schuster Special Sales at 1-866-506-1949 or business@simonandschuster.com.

The Simon & Schuster Speakers Bureau can bring authors to your live event. For more information or to book an event, contact the Simon & Schuster Speakers Bureau at 1-866-248-3049 or visit our website at www.simonspeakers.com.

Interior design by Lewelin Polanco

Manufactured in the United States of America

1   3   5   7   9   10   8   6   4   2

Library of Congress Cataloging-in-Publication Data
Names: DeSteno, David, author.
Title: How God works : the science behind the benefits of religion / David DeSteno.
Description: New York : Simon & Schuster, [2021] | Includes bibliographical references and index.
Identifiers: LCCN 2021020294 (print) | LCCN 2021020295 (ebook) | ISBN 9781982142315 | ISBN 9781982142322 (paperback) | ISBN 9781982142339 (ebook)
Subjects: LCSH: Psychology, Religious. | Psychology and religion.
Classification: LCC BL53 .D375 2021 (print) | LCC BL53 (ebook) | DDC 200.1/9—dc23
LC record available at https://lccn.loc.gov/2021020294
LC ebook record available at https://lccn.loc.gov/2021020295

ISBN 978-1-9821-4231-5
ISBN 978-1-9821-4233-9 (ebook)

To my family

Contents

Contents

A Note on Pronouns

When you write about God, pronouns can be a problem. I thought about using "they," as it is now frequently done when one is uncertain of the gender or to include all possible genders. But when writing about different religions, some of which have a single deity and some of which have multiple, that also proved confusing. Ultimately, I settled on a two-part strategy, one that I hope you'll understand as showing respect both for the unknowable nature of God(s) and for specific religions' views of the divine. When I'm discussing God or gods in general, I'll use "It" and "they," respectively. But when I'm discussing the deity of a specific religion, I'll use the pronoun that faith typically applies.

Introduction
The Journey Ahead

How do you raise a child to be a good person? What are your responsibilities to your family, your friends, and your community? How do you cope with a serious illness? Can you find someone to love and, if you do, how do you go on when they're gone? How do you find joy and meaning in life—especially in difficult times—and how do you make sense of your life's inevitable end?

These are the questions that keep people up at night. They strike at the heart of what it means to be human. And so they keep me up at night too. Not only because I'm trying to figure out, like millions of others, how to live a good life. But also because for the past thirty years my career has focused on uncovering ways to help people become more moral, more compassionate, and more resilient as they walk the road of life.

That might be surprising, as I'm not a priest, therapist, or life coach. I'm a research scientist. I conduct psychological experiments. And few people would expect to find the meaning of life through scientific investigation and lab work.

For millennia, most people have turned to priests, ministers, rabbis, and imams to help them deal with grief and loss, birth and death, morality and meaning. And many still turn to a traditional faith or seek out new modes of spirituality to address the challenges and opportunities that life presents.

But over the past few decades, science has started finding ways to help people deal with these issues too. Psychologists like me study things like generosity, empathy, resilience, and forgiveness. And as scientists learn more about what helps foster these feelings and behaviors, we can also suggest practical steps that people can take to improve their lives.

This data-driven approach may seem at odds with religion. Indeed, even though I was raised Catholic, for most of my adult life, I didn't pay religion much heed. Like many scientists, I assumed it was irrelevant to my work.

Yet, over the years, as I continued to scientifically study the questions that fascinated me—questions about how to improve the human condition—I was surprised that many of the answers I found aligned with religious ideas. Even more surprising to me was that certain aspects of religious practices, even when removed from their spiritual settings, had a profound impact on people's minds.

My research team found, for example, that giving thanks to one person (or to God) made people more honest and generous to others—not only to those they cared about but also to strangers. We saw that just a few weeks of meditation made people more compassionate—more willing to jump out of their seats to aid others in pain and to resist lashing out at people who might otherwise provoke them to violence. To our surprise, we found that even basic parts of many religious rituals, like moving or singing together, made people feel more connected and committed to one another.

Other researchers have discovered that religious practices can lessen anxiety, reduce depression, and even increase physical health. In fact, much of what psychologists and neuroscientists were finding about how to change people's beliefs, feelings, and behaviors—how to support them when they grieve, how to help them find connection and happiness—seemed to echo ideas and techniques that religions have been using for thousands of years. To my growing curiosity, I realized that we scientists were "discovering" many things that others had realized and implemented long ago.

That's when it dawned on me: we were going about this in the wrong way. I realized that the surprise my colleagues and I felt when we saw evidence of religion's benefits was a sign of our hubris—born of a common notion among scientists: all of religion was superstition and, therefore, could have little practical benefit. Yet, as I learned and as this book shows, spiritual leaders often understood—in ways that we can now scientifically confirm—how to help people live better. Social scientists are the new kids on the block.

Ironically, around the time I started having these thoughts, a larger cultural battle between science and religion was again heating up. Fundamentalist faiths were casting science as a misguided or even malevolent source of information. Prominent scientists were arguing the reverse: religion wasn't only wrong, it was dangerous. The New Atheist movement, led by eminent thinkers like Richard Dawkins, Daniel Dennett, Steven Pinker, and Sam Harris, cast religion almost as a plague on the enlightened mind.

But when I looked at the results of my studies and those of other researchers, I saw a more nuanced relationship between science and religion. I saw two approaches to understanding how to improve people's lives that frequently complemented each other.

Don't get me wrong. I firmly believe that the scientific method is a wonder. It's a framework that offers one of the best ways to test ideas about how the world works. But when it comes to thinking about how to help people through life's travails, we scientists shouldn't be starting from scratch. Just as ancient doesn't always mean wise, neither does it always mean naïve.

I believe this view makes intuitive sense. When it comes to managing the human experience, it would be strange if thousands of years of religious thought didn't have much to offer. As I said, people have long turned to spiritual leaders and religious communities for guidance about how to live well. And even in our increasingly secular era, there's a good reason why people still do. Across the globe, those who regularly take part in religious practices report greater well-being than those who don't. The key point here, though, is easy to miss. Saying you're religious doesn't matter much for health and happiness. It's *being* religious—taking part in the rituals and practices of a faith—that makes life better.

If we remove the theology—views about the nature of God, the creation of the universe, and the like—from the day-to-day practice of religious faith, most of the debates that stoke animosity between science and religion evaporate. What we're left with is a series of rituals, customs, and sentiments that are themselves the results of experiments of sorts. Over thousands of years, these experiments, carried out in the messy thick of life as opposed to sterile labs, have led to the design of what we might call spiritual technologies—tools and processes meant to sooth, move, convince, or otherwise tweak the mind. It's here, in the repetition of prayer, the stillness of contemplation, the joining of hands in celebration or sorrow, the dancing, singing, writhing, and swaying, that—actually or metaphorically, depending on your view—we can see God at work. To ignore that body of knowledge is to slow the progress of science itself and limit its potential benefit to humanity.

But before we can start down this path, we need to remove a potential roadblock.

-Isms Just Get in the Way

Theism, deism, atheism. When it comes to religion, adopting most any -ism save agnosticism requires you to embrace a narrow view about God. If you're a theist, you believe in a particular god of the intervening type—one willing to have a relationship with you and to whom you can appeal. If you're a deist, you believe God created the universe, but is now rather hands-off. If you're an atheist, there is no God, plain and simple. We're all here based on the rules of physics, biology, and fortunate rolls of the probabilistic dice that continually unfolded after the big bang. And if you're an agnostic, you choose not to choose.

It's important to realize, though, that whichever -ism you abide by—even atheism—depends in part on faith. If you choose to be an atheist, it's a faith in the principles of science—faith that chance favored us in this corner of the cosmos. Even Richard Dawkins, probably the most well-known advocate for the absence of God's hand in creation, freely admits that he can't be absolutely certain that God doesn't exist. As there's no agreed-upon scientific test for God's fingerprint, it's a question that no amount of empirical analysis can answer. And so, even for the most strident atheist, belief that God doesn't exist is a matter of faith, not a provable fact.

It's a similar case for religious theologies. When they seem absolutely contradicted by what we see in the world, they can be difficult to defend. For this reason, many religions have become more open to science as the centuries progressed. The Catholic Church, but one example of many, now teaches that science can enrich human understanding of life on earth, even in ways that challenge strict interpretations of its own texts. Catholics, for instance, are encouraged to take the biblical Book of Genesis as a metaphorical tale, should they so choose. Tibetan Buddhists take a similar stance. The Dalai Lama has been consistently open to science as a source of knowledge, so much so that he regularly funds studies of the neurological effects of meditation. He even once said that if science can prove reincarnation doesn't exist, Tibetan Buddhists would abandon the notion. Of course, he then quipped he didn't think that definitive evidence would emerge anytime soon.

Like other ideological labels we use—liberal, conservative, libertarian, socialist—religious -isms can usefully identify our beliefs. But they can also cut down on conversation if we adhere to them too single-mindedly. Just because we disagree in our overarching political philosophy doesn't mean we should assume we disagree about every government policy; there may be ample common ground. The same goes for our religious beliefs. Atheists and Buddhists might disagree about whether reincarnation is real, for instance, but agree about the value of meditation or how to help people mourn.

So, for now at least, I'd ask you to put your -isms to the side. There's no need to abandon them; each of us has a right to our own notions about God. But for what I'm going to focus on in this book—investigating how religious technologies can help support people throughout their lives—most of these -isms don't matter. Understanding how a technology was developed isn't always necessary to use it. You don't need to know how the microchips in your cell phone work or even who developed them in order to connect with friends across the country. The same applies to religious rituals and practices.

I'm not saying that what you believe doesn't matter. As we'll see in this book, it certainly does. What I am saying is that trying to figure out how and why the tools of religion work on the mind doesn't require solving the problem of whether God exists and directed their development. All you need is a willingness to put these techniques and practices to a test: Do they alter how we act, how we feel, how healthy and how happy we are? And if they do, how can we adapt them to even better advantage? -Isms don't help us answer these questions; in fact, they mostly get in the way.

I want to be clear that I'm not an apologist for religion. My goal isn't to argue that religion is always good. I fully recognize that religious beliefs have been used to motivate and justify horrendous acts of violence and abuse, to perpetuate many types of discrimination and inequality, and to push people toward many kinds of irrational behavior.

But, as with most technologies, religion's value depends on the intentions of those using it. Yes, some of the tools religions provide can be used for evil purposes. But that's not a reason to indict the entire enterprise, especially when there's ample evidence that other items in religion's toolbox can help foster people's noblest traits.

Spiritual technologies, like any other effective technologies, are powerful. They can destroy societies or strengthen them. That's why we need to understand how we can better use the helpful tools while combating the harmful ones.

Tools of the Trade

Rituals are observable practices that help define a religion. Some are done daily, some weekly, some yearly, and some (like funerals and weddings) only at specific points in life. And while many might feel quite familiar to us, trying to define exactly what makes something a ritual is tricky. Some use symbols; some don't. Some involve spoken prayers; others are conducted silently. Some even seem to mimic ordinary parts of life: What makes not eating for a day different from a religious fast? What makes lighting a candle at Shabbat—the Jewish weekly day of rest—different from lighting a candle when the power goes out?

The best definition of "ritual" I've seen comes from the eminent religion scholar Catherine Bell. Rituals, she argues, are a set of actions designed to be special—to highlight, differentiate, and privilege what is being done. Making certain acts feel formal, using symbols, evoking emotion, using repetition—these all are potential ways to mark that specialness. None of them are strictly necessary, though. Just by declaring that certain acts are special, we make them meaningful. They draw our attention, imagination, and sometimes hopes, in a way that mere habits don't. And as such, they change the way that otherwise mundane actions speak to our minds.

At heart, almost all rituals seek to bring about change. By altering how our minds encode and process information, the ways we move our bodies in space and in relation to others, and the values and expectations we place on ourselves and those around us, rituals regulate our beliefs, our behaviors, and our bonds with others. In so doing, they help us experience joy, manage pain, persevere toward difficult goals, and bounce back from painful losses.

We humans have always strived to develop technologies that give us some control, or at least a feeling of control, over the challenges that life throws at us. In a secular context, one way to do this is via psychology. Researchers like me devote our professional lives to figuring out why people think and feel what they do, and, and in cases where those thoughts or actions are undesirable, to helping people change. We conduct experiments to see whether a certain type of drug or therapy alleviates anxiety or pain. We test "nudges," such as policies that require people to opt in or opt out of a program, in an effort to help them save for retirement or become an organ donor. We design and evaluate social and dating algorithms and platforms to help connect people who might otherwise feel isolated. All the while, we aim to satisfy people's urgent desires for science-backed life hacks that will make them smarter, healthier, and happier.

This is all great. We're lucky to be living at a time when the rate of discovery and the flow of information has never been quicker. But for thousands of years, humans have gone about developing tools outside of the strict scientific method. We've experimented, but in a more colloquial sense of the term. Put simply, we've tried things that, in some way, seemed promising to us and waited to see what happened. That's the way many religious rituals have come about. Change features prominently even among established religions. Elements of worship are modernized. The numerous sects and denominations in Christianity, Islam, Judaism, and Buddhism all derive from change and evolution within those faiths—change that's reflected not only in their dogmas but also in their practices.

But new rituals can emerge even more quickly than that. In Silicon Valley, a company called the Ritual Design Lab posts a promising slogan on its website: "You tell us your problem. We will make you a ritual." It's no fly-by-night; its customers include Microsoft, Airbnb, and SAP. It even offers an app, IdeaPOP, that will help you create your own rituals.

In a similar vein, if you need a ritual to help prepare for the emotional challenges of a preventative mastectomy, a prayer for refugee children living in camps, or guidance on a funeral ceremony for a beloved pet, the Ritualwell website offers suggestions coming from the Jewish Reconstructionist movement. Certain of these will appeal to many; others may not. But the ones that do—the ones that work—will grow in use.

Science has come to recognize the special power of rituals. Recent experiments have shown that even an arbitrary set of actions, when ritualized, can help people. Take dieting, for example. Researchers invited people trying to lose weight to take part in a five-day experiment. They told half the people that when getting ready to eat, they first had to cut their food into several pieces, then rearrange the pieces on their plates so that they formed a symmetrical pattern, and then finally tap their utensil on each piece of food three times before they took a bite. They asked the other half simply to think about what they were eating in a careful way.

Surprising as it may seem, for every one of those five days, people who performed the prescribed ritual consumed 224 fewer calories on average than those who actually stopped to think about what they were eating. Something similar happened even when the researchers tempted health-conscious people with chocolate versus carrots. Those who performed a ritual—this time knocking on a table, taking deep breaths, and closing their eyes—were 25 percent more likely to select a carrot to eat than to take a chocolate candy. Here again, a ritual created on the spot helped people improve their self-control.

These surely aren't the best rituals to help people diet or fast. They simply offer proof that some types of ritual actions can affect our desires and behaviors. The big question, of course, is: Which ones? Which rituals—which combinations of elements—work best? And it's here that religions have a vast head start. They've "debugged" the technologies they've used through the centuries.

No ritual is perfect at the outset. But they have to start somewhere. So people often begin by making choices that are informed by theology and symbolism. The resulting mix is a set of practices that often combines beliefs, songs, prayers, or movements that speak to the mind and body on several different levels—some of which we understand and others of which we don't. But over time, rituals change to sharpen their effects, leading to that debugging I just mentioned.

Buddhists, for example, have developed different meditation

practices for different purposes. Some are meant to enhance attention, others to cultivate compassion. But in each case, tweaks were made over time in line with how well they achieved the desired ends. Even among very centralized and hierarchical religions like Catholicism, changes that come from the top are meant to better serve the needs of the faithful.

Given the ubiquity and variety of religious rituals and practices, it's surprising that science hasn't taken up the charge to examine their effects more widely and carefully. One exception over the past decade has been mindfulness. We now know, with ample data to back it up, that meditation offers many benefits. It enhances attention, decreases anxiety and stress, and even increases compassionate behavior toward others. But none of that would be news to the spiritual thinkers who developed contemplative techniques centuries ago. That's what they set out to do in the first place.

There's no reason to think that meditation is the only practice created by religion that might have scientifically verifiable benefits. It's one tool among many that several traditions have used. We only recognize its benefits because the Dalai Lama encouraged scientists to study it. He gave it a head start. The question we should be asking, then, is: What's the next mindfulness? What's the next spiritual technology that we can use to improve people's lives? It's out there if we're willing to look.

Religioprospecting

This book sets out to do with religion what has been done successfully in other realms to dramatically improve human life. Consider the field of medicine. For decades, pharmaceutical science has looked to traditional healing for medicines and insights that might help treat ailments. In the mid-twentieth century, for example, scientists had the technical ability to produce new pharmaceuticals, but not enough ideas about exactly which ones to produce. So many drug companies sent their scientists bioprospecting—looking for folk remedies from cultures around the world they could bring back to their labs to test.

In the 1950s, the researcher Gordon Svoboda, working for Eli Lilly, added rosy periwinkle—an evergreen shrub adorned with delicate, five-petal, pink flowers—to a list of compounds to be examined. Although originally native to Madagascar, the plant had spread through commerce to Southeast Asia, Europe, and Jamaica in the 1700s and 1800s, and many cultures touted its power to combat diabetes. Interested in the possibility, the scientists at Lilly set to work examining the plant's chemical makeup.

The plant did indeed contain chemicals that helped the body regulate blood sugar (although these weren't found until much later). But two other compounds really sparked the scientists' interest. These compounds—vincristine and vinblastine—appeared to destroy proliferations of white blood cells—proliferations common to cancers like leukemia and Hodgkin's lymphoma. Through continued testing and development, scientists refined these compounds into medications that helped increase the survival rate for these cancers from 10 percent to 90 percent.

There's a plethora of examples like this one, where older, traditional notions informed the development of effective new treatments. But if those scientists weren't willing to look at traditional ideas for healing, they might have missed the opportunity to find potentially powerful treatments. That's as true today as it was in the 1950s. Such bioprospecting isn't the only way to find cures, of course, but it's proven to be a very effective one.

While most people are open to prospecting for new biologics to heal the body and brain, that same open-mindedness doesn't extend to psychologics. By "psychologics," I mean the beliefs, practices, and rituals that affect human minds. Just as various cultures may have found chemical tools to enhance biological well-being, so, too, might they have found psychological ones—ones that they've embedded in their spiritual contexts. Again, the origin of such tools isn't germane to determining how useful they are. Whether or not one believes that God put rosy periwinkle on earth to help Its creatures heal themselves doesn't affect its ability to fight cancer. What led to this lifesaving discovery was openness to an idea followed by a careful evaluation of the evidence.

The time for religioprospecting has come. As with biologics, the promise of some practices may be just that: promises without any evidence of effect. But many others will, like the traditional remedies from which some modern medicines spring, surprise us in their efficacy and even suggest new uses.

There's a simple reason why I believe this view is correct: convergence. No matter where or when we live, the path of life, for most, winds past the same landmarks. We're born. We grow into a community and learn its rules. We become adults and look for someone with whom to connect. We love. We raise families. We age. We get sick. We grieve for those we lose, and we face the prospect of our own demise. For millennia, it's been this way. And for each of these mileposts—each of these points of meaning, joy, or dread—religions the world over have devised rituals and practices to help us through.

Every faith has a ceremony to welcome a new life into the community, a set of practices to instill morality in the young and to transition them to adulthood, rituals to bind people together, to quell their anxieties, to heal their bodies, to console their souls, and to ease their demise. More than 80 percent of the world's population identifies to a degree with some religion, thereby continuing an embrace of the tools such traditions provide.

In the pages that follow, I invite you to walk that path of life with me. To see what various religions have already discovered about how to help us traverse it more successfully. Along the way, we'll find remarkable similarities in the tools religions offer, but perhaps even more important, some striking differences between them. Yes, every religion prescribes practices for birth and death, but that doesn't mean that all are equally effective. Might Shinto rituals before and after a baby's birth lead to better outcomes for mother and child than the birth rituals of other religions? Might the Jewish practice of sitting shiva better ease the pain of a grieving family than rituals of other faiths? Questions like these can be answered only if we start to examine religious practices with a scientific eye.

Using the tools science provides—experimentation, data analysis, and more—we can set aside debates about the theological meanings of rituals and focus instead on how they influence the body and mind. Why, for example, can contemplating death by placing ashes on your forehead or meditating in front of a corpse make you more compassionate? Why can a healer's touch reduce pain? Why can covering the mirrors in a home during times of mourning reduce feelings of grief?

We'll explore how rituals, practices, and sentiments from the world's religions nudge our minds in certain ways. In some cases, research on specific religious ideas and practices already exists. In others, I'll break down the component parts of religious beliefs and rituals to show how they align with what psychology and neuroscience know about how our minds work. And through this process, I'll offer insights into how certain aspects of rituals and practices might be adapted to help both secular people and those of different faiths improve their well-being.

Along this path of discovery, two themes will appear time and again: belief and connection. Since these play an essential role in religion's influence on our health and happiness at all points in life, I want to highlight them here before we begin our journey.

The Balm of Belief

In the developed world, most people live a life infused with the luxury of choice. The grocery store offers approximately forty-seven different types of cereal. The television, two hundred or more channels of programming. Dating apps, more profiles than people can possibly swipe. But perhaps what we think of as a luxury might be anything but. Choice, and the uncertainties that accompany it, can actually be a curse at times.

One of the most important insights to emerge from neuroscience over the past two decades is that the human mind is a kind of prediction machine. It's built not simply to respond to stimuli but rather to anticipate them. What makes the mind so adaptive and efficient is its ability to guess what's coming next. And although we can't be certain of the characteristics of all animal minds, it's probably safe to say that humans are among the few species, if not the only one, that can effectively time travel in this way. We can simulate the future, running all types of scenarios in our heads. We can also relive the past in exquisite detail, meaning we can reexperience the pleasures or regrets resulting from all the choices we've made.

The fact that choice can be a bane may sound strange, as most people think that more choices will make it more likely that we'll find the option that's tailored exactly to our needs. Yet, while that may be true in terms of maximizing a specific outcome, it's not the case in terms of maximizing overall well-being. As psychologists have repeatedly shown, having too many choices can cause greater dissatisfaction with whatever option we ultimately choose.

It's precisely because we don't want to make the wrong choice that having too many options can push us into choice paralysis. Trying to analyze everything can become overwhelming when the options in front of us grow beyond a select few. The psychologist Barry Schwartz has repeatedly shown that those of us he calls maximizers—the ones who always want to find the single best option in any situation—tend to be less happy, less optimistic, and more prone to depression and regret than are others who feel that good enough options will do.

While these are important findings about how the mind works, you might wonder what they have to do with religion. Think of it this way. If running simulations and having regrets about which toaster or car to buy can make us feel bad—a fact for which there's ample evidence—what happens when we're considering weightier subjects? What if you're deciding whom to marry? Or whether lying to save your job is okay? Or what you should do to help your child recover from an illness? Uncertainty in the realms of morality and fate—the realms that religions dominate for many people—is taxing not only because it requires the brain to simulate so many options but also because of the emotional consequences involved. And it's here, as we'll see, that belief comes into play. With belief—that God will intervene, that a ritual will heal, that a choice never to lie or cheat ensures the best outcomes—comes certainty. And with certainty comes a kind of inner peace.

The links between faith and decreased anxiety can even be seen at the neurological level. For example, scientists have shown how belief calms activity in the anterior cingulate cortex (ACC)—a part of the brain associated with what we might call "alarm bell" experiences. When we feel annoyed or threatened, certain patterns of activity in the ACC intensify. These are the same patterns that ramp up in those suffering from anxiety disorders, and they're also ones that are reduced by alcohol and medications like Valium and Xanax.

When neuroscientists measured activity in the ACC as people were confronted with decisions in which they made errors, those who had stronger belief in God showed less activity than did others. In other words, believers showed less anxiety at the neurological level about making perfect choices. In a similar vein, researchers also found that letting believers reflect on their faith before making decisions further reduced ACC activity in the face of errors. Simply put, thinking about God made religious people calmer.

The upshot is pretty clear: the sense of certainty that comes from religious belief dials down the brain's response to error and uncertainty in all areas. The ACC's "alarm bells" are less intense, and choices are made with less regret. This is one reason, among many, why research consistently links religious belief to decreased stress in daily life.

Belief doesn't make people more complacent or less intelligent. It simply reduces the revved-up, hypervigilant, hypercritical state many of us fall into as we strive to make complicated decisions. Throughout this book, we'll see how enhanced belief, and the certainty it brings, can be fostered through religious practices and rituals.

Loneliness Is Hell

A second theme we'll see that rituals address in people's lives is connection. For humans, there are few states worse than loneliness. We are social beings. We crave the company of others. We thrive by working with and supporting one another.

Without strong connections to another person, we pay a heavy price. Loneliness is as dangerous as smoking in terms of its potential to shorten people's lives. It impairs immunity, worsens inflammation, and increases blood pressure, all of which are linked to maladies like heart disease and diabetes.

It's precisely because of these dangerous changes to our health that our brains, even during early stages of isolation, make us experience loneliness as actual pain. Religion, like many social institutions, can combat this pain by giving people opportunities to come together. For example, most religions prescribe obligatory gatherings. But unlike other social institutions, religions' power to create connection isn't limited to scheduling. Religions can also forge meaningful bonds through the power of the rituals themselves. Although we'll see many examples of such binding happening later in this book, let me offer one now as evidence of this fact.

What psychologists call motor synchrony—moving parts of your body in time with others—is a part of many rituals the world over. Sometimes it's bowing and swaying, sometimes it's spinning and dancing, and sometimes it's joint singing and praying. But however the movements in question take place, they're a marker to the brain that the people involved are parts of a larger whole. Their outcomes are joined. It's such a fundamental signal of being joined together that infants as young as fifteen months of age already use it as a cue to determine who is linked to whom.

To show the effects of synchronous movement, my lab conducted an experiment where we paired each person with a partner and had them put on headphones and tap their hands to the beats they heard. While neither member of each pair in the experiment knew the other, some pairs heard synchronized beats and thus tapped in time with each other. Other pairs heard random beats that led to no synchronization at all. Following the tapping, we asked each pair how similar they felt to their partner. As we anticipated, those who had tapped in time felt a greater link to each other. And when we later orchestrated a situation where one member of the pair needed help completing a difficult task, partners who had tapped synchronously were much more likely to come to the aid of each other and offer assistance (a rate of 49 percent) than were partners who didn't (a rate of 18 percent). One simple act of synchronized movement was all it took to make people feel connected enough to almost triple their rate for helping a complete stranger. Many other researchers have found similar results.

Experiments like these prove that a common element of ritual, even when stripped bare of any theological trappings, can still speak to the mind on a deep level. But that doesn't mean combining the more basic elements of ritual with religious belief can't enhance their power even more. In compelling work, a team of researchers from New Zealand's Victoria University of Wellington set out to see if synchronous movement could have an even greater effect if it was religiously inspired.

The researchers measured feelings of connection, trust, and actual cooperation between people before and after they engaged in a type of chant associated with their faith, more secular synchronous acts like drumming or singing nonreligious songs together, or activities like playing poker that people do together without any synchronous movement. Although the researchers found that synchrony of any type made people feel closer to, trust, and cooperate more with one another, most of these effects were magnified when the synchrony had a sacred element attached to it—that is, when people chanted in a manner that followed a ritual of their faith. Put another way, a belief that this activity was spiritually meaningful—that, in accord with Bell's definition of "ritual," it was a special as opposed to mundane activity—intensified the impact that synchrony had on people's minds.

Unlike regularly participating in a religion's rituals, these experiments involved a single act of synchrony. So while their ability to create bonds between people was evident, the magnitude and longevity of such bonds are likely to be even greater when they're repeated regularly while attending services together.

Religions the world over appear to have converged on synchrony as a tool for creating connection. Centuries before psychologists ever studied it, almost every tradition had adopted it as a way to bind people together—to nudge them to support one another and to reduce the toll loneliness can take on the body and mind.

Of course, synchrony is but one of many tools religions use to build connection. The greater point I want to make is that religions have identified effective technologies that need to be studied in the rich context in which they're used (as opposed to the more constrained settings of the lab) if we're to fully appreciate how they can reinforce each other—how beliefs, symbols, actions, and group behavior can work synergistically to magnify each other's impact. It's here that religions have a long head start. It's here that they're playing a psychological symphony, not just randomly striking single notes we find soothing.

Setting Out

With all this in mind, it's time to begin our journey along life's path, examining how the world's religions try to ease our way. Beginning with the challenges birth presents to parents and infants, we'll move on to see how rituals also guide the development of morality in the formative years of childhood, how they help us cross the thresholds from childhood into adolescence and adulthood, how they aid us in finding a loving connection to each other and perhaps even to something greater, how they heal our minds and bodies as we move through midlife, and, finally, how they help us cope with the loss of loved ones and our own inevitable ends.

Along the way, I'll point out not only the incredible convergences across faiths—a testament to the shared challenges all humans face—but also, as I suggested above, how some faiths may have honed their technologies in even more targeted ways. It's not that the rituals of any one faith are generally superior to those of others, but rather that for specific challenges, some may have found tweaks or solutions that push the mind's buttons more effectively.

As I make these points, my goal isn't to provide a completely comprehensive view of rituals from across the globe. That would take many books. Instead, I've selected examples from both the world's major religions and its more localized faiths that show most clearly how religion can benefit us at various points in our lives. You might notice that I focus somewhat more on the rites of the major faiths. This isn't because I see them as intrinsically better in any way, but because they address some issues that hold greater importance for people living in more complex, modern societies (which itself is one reason why they've spread around the world). Morality is one. It's not easy to behave badly when you live in a small village. But in larger cities, greater anonymity makes it easier to cheat or steal. Existential crises are another. If your life is primarily focused on surviving from day to day, you often don't have the luxury of pondering the meaning of life or worrying if you're on the right path.

So let's set out.

Infancy: Welcoming
and Binding

*A*llah *is most great. I bear witness that there is none worthy of being worshipped except Allah. I bear witness that Muhammad is the apostle of Allah. Come to prayer. Come to success.*

Whether in the hospital, or more traditionally surrounded by female family and friend attendants at home, these are the first words that a Muslim child hears moments after birth. As the infant is presented to its father for the first time, he cradles it adoringly and recites these words, which constitute part of the *adhan*, or Muslim call to prayer, into the child's right ear.

A few moments afterward, another honored family member or friend rubs a small piece of softened date or other sweet treat on the infant's upper palate—a ritual known as the *tahneek*. The symbolism of this action is twofold. Traditionally, the person offering the date had first softened it in their own mouth, so passing their saliva to the infant marked a hope that their noble traits would pass as well. The second symbolism of *tahneek* is the hope that the treat would bode good fortune for the child's coming life—a life to be filled with sweet things.

As beautiful as birth is, it marks one of the biggest changes in life. For infants, it's the start of a journey. For parents, it's a reset of sorts—an event that will fundamentally change their routines and priorities. And while everyone involved wants this new life to be a success, that success is by no means guaranteed. It will require a mix of sacrifice and support to bring it to fruition.

Our success in the first few years of life boils down to gaining acceptance, both from our parents and by the larger web of people who surround us. The more practical and emotional sustenance our parents give us, the better off we'll be throughout our lives. And the more favorably our community looks upon us, the better chance we'll have for support in the short and long term.

Fortunately, we humans come equipped with tools for ingratiating ourselves to others right from the start. Hormonal responses, the specific sound of cries, and even babies' physical appearances all help to elicit care from parents and welcoming smiles form passersby. Babies are cute for a reason. Their rounded features evoke an instinctual affection in most people—even strangers.

Biology isn't destiny, though. Sometimes it goes wrong or just isn't strong enough on its own to create and maintain the support growing babes need to thrive. Sometimes parents can face a lot of stress or anxiety that impedes their ability to connect with a new child. Sometimes they're just burned out or not willing to give as much time, attention, or support to their child as they could. Sometimes, especially for someone who isn't a parent, appreciating the specialness and potential of any infant can be difficult. They're squishy, demanding blobs, after all.

Here's where the spiritual technologies that surround birth come into play. Whichever faith they come from—Muslim, Christian,

Shinto, or the like—they all serve one overarching goal: to boost any infant's odds. Although the symbols and practices may differ a bit, these practices work to help parents provide the support their new young ones need and to help the community see why they should welcome these babies into their midst. As the Muslim *adhan* states explicitly: by coming to prayer and services—by adopting these technologies—people will be coming to success. That's as true at the beginning of life as it is later on.

Tending Comes First

Shinto is the national religion of Japan, and most Japanese practice it to some extent. The word *shinto* means "the way of the gods," and Shinto practice centers on belief in kami—spirits that inhabit natural places and living beings.

In Shinto, the birth of a child is a gift of the kami, and throughout the early years of its life, the rituals focus parents not only on caring for and celebrating their child but also on gratitude for their existence. The child is so prized that ritualized care for it starts well before its birth. During the fifth month of pregnancy, Japanese mothers-to-be celebrate the *obiiwai*—the ritual of sash binding. Here, a close female relative ties a beautiful cotton belt around the expectant mother's belly to provide gentle support, warmth, and protection for the growing child it cradles. Often, *obiiwai* takes places in Shinto shrines but it can be performed in the home as well. The ritual also involves prayers for the coming child's welfare. The sash itself also serves as a reminder of the responsibilities of motherhood. It marks the symbolic start of caretaking.

Assuming all goes well at birth, the next ritual Shinto prescribes is *oshichiya*, or the naming ceremony. On the seventh evening after a child is born, the parents invite family and friends to take part in a joyous meal, traditionally consisting of sea bream (a fish whose name in Japanese is a homonym of the word for joy) and rice with red beans. Up to now, the family may have been using a silly nickname to refer to the baby, but on this evening the parents formally announce the true name to everyone and begin to use it. To mark the specialness of the occasion and the pride they take in their new little one, who is traditionally dressed in white, they also ceremonially write the child's name using calligraphy on special white paper that they then hang on the wall. This celebration formally begins the child's introduction to the world beyond its home.

After a month, the family takes part in *omiyamairi*: the infant's first visit to a Shinto shrine. Parents and babies dress their best for this, which for the baby means buying another new outfit and a special kimono to wrap it in. Traditionally, it's the paternal grandmother who carries the child into the shrine, as Japanese custom suggests that mothers need to rest as much as possible after giving birth.

Once inside, the Shinto priest will wave an *onusa*—a stick with dozens of billowing papers attached to it—from side to side to purify everyone before using another sacred rod with bells attached to it to remove the influence of any evil spirits from the child. Throughout all of this, the priests also thank the kami for the child's birth and beseech them to protect the child and give it good fortune. *Omiyamari*, like many Shinto rites around a child's early years, also entails a significant cost for the parents. Besides the expense for the new clothes and kimono, the parents also are expected to make a sizable donation to the shrine and to provide commemorative gifts to everyone who attended.

Next, when the child is about four months old, the family celebrates *okuizome*: the first bite of food. Since it's not a great idea to feed adult food to kids that age, the meal is largely symbolic.

Infancy

The parents first purchase an expensive red (for boys) or black (for girls) set of dishware and then prepare a traditional Japanese meal, again consisting of sea bream, red beans and rice, but also pickled vegetables and soup. Small bits are then pretend-fed to the child while the larger family enjoys the banquet in earnest.

When the first March 3 for girls or May 5 for boys rolls around, it's time for *hatsuzekku*. As with the earlier rituals, the focus here is on celebrating the child and expressing gratitude that he or she has, hopefully, been growing in size and strength. Girls receive *hina*—ornamental dolls representing the royal family and court. For boys, the home is decorated with samurai figures and armor. Here, too, the larger family often gathers for celebratory meals provided by the young one's parents.

When it's time for a child's first birthday, there's yet another ritual celebration. Here, parents put sticky rice patties, a sacred Shinto food, in a pouch on the baby's back while the child tries to walk with the added weight. The goal isn't to weigh them down but to transfer power to them.

No matter how you count it, that's a very busy first year! But it's not where Shinto's ritual celebrations of children ends. At three, five, and seven years of age, *shichigosan* is celebrated—a ritual in which children are again dressed in traditional clothes and taken to shrines for prayers and blessings that express appreciation for their development and ask for continued good fortune. With each, parents again face costs in terms of time and money. There are new clothes to buy, donations to make, and meals to provide for family and friends.

Almost all of the world's religions include rituals similar to Shinto's *oshichiya* and *omiyamairi*. For Hindus, the name-giving ceremony known as *namakarana* usually occurs around the twelfth day after birth and centers on family and friends gathering while a parent, led by a priest, writes the child's name on a piece of paper (to be sanctified by the priest) and then whispers it into the child's ear before announcing it to all. In Islam, the naming ceremony known as the *aqiqah* takes place a week after the child's birth. Christians baptize their babies. That ceremony doesn't reveal the child's name per se, but the priest does highlight the name while blessing the new arrival with holy water. Jews hold a brief ceremony in which an infant's Hebrew name is announced to the congregation at temple.

This convergence of rites for naming and blessing across religions anticipates a truth more recently discovered by psychologists and other scientists. We don't name what we don't value, and giving something or someone a name confers value upon it. At the most basic psychological level, a specific name, as opposed to a generic label like "baby," implies that something has a mind; it has agency. And whatever has agency—whatever can think and feel—is worthy of our concern. Its joys and its pains matter, even if it doesn't yet have the ability to express them.

Just giving or recognizing that something has a name makes us feel more empathetic toward it. Pets are a great example, but it even works for mundane, mindless objects. Your car, your computer, even a cucumber. Research has shown that many people's brains respond differently to the piercing of a vegetable that has been given a human name. Via brain imaging, we can see that people show greater signs of empathic distress when vegetables that have been named Bob or Sue get pricked with a needle compared to when their unnamed counterparts get stuck on the cutting board.

A name serves not only as a form of identification, but as a marker of moral worth. And giving or announcing a name as part of a ritual stands as a public way of reinforcing that value. It's an additional reminder to people, especially those beyond the immediate family, that a baby—a wriggly lump of flesh who can't even look anyone in the eye—is nonetheless a being capable of feeling who deserves the community's respect and protection. It's also why many faiths encourage parents to name their children after saints, respected family members, and the like. Those names are associated with virtues—virtues that come to mind and color impressions of the seeming blank slates that infants present.

You can also see the psychological power of naming in another way: its reverse. The process of dehumanization often begins by refusing to call people by their names. Referring to people by a number, or calling them pigs or dogs, is a first step many regimes have used to enable later cruelty. When you remove people's names, you automatically inhibit the normal empathy we'd feel for them. This is also why we don't name the animals we intend to eat.

The rites of Shinto, though, go much beyond naming rituals. And while it's not the only religion that has some additional rites surrounding the early years of a child's life, the front-loaded package it offers is exceptional in the ways it focuses parents on tending to and embracing the value of their children in a very costly public way.

Since a child depends on its parents for *everything*, quickly developing a strong bond between the two is an essential ingredient for their health and well-being, both in the moment and in the long run. Children who grow up without strong and nurturing relationships with their parents have trouble forming friendships and romantic relationships, and they're more susceptible to depression, anxiety, and related illness later in life. Put simply, not receiving consistent parental care and warmth sets a child up for failure. For this reason, our bodies come equipped with a suite of tools meant to help us rapidly form deep attachments with infants.

During birth and the months that follow, hormones flood a mother's brain to help ensure that this needy, crying, helpless human evokes love rather than ire or indifference. Fathers, too, get a hormone boost: their levels of oxytocin, which is central to forming bonds, rise when they hold or play with their child. But, for some parents—20 percent to 30 percent, depending on the survey—the hormonal boost just isn't enough to make the love flow. Try as they might, they can't connect with their baby. And even for the 80 percent who can connect, maintaining their devotion during sleepless nights, constant cleanup, and the many other trials of new parenthood can often be a challenge. Yet, as Alison Gopnik, one of the world's leading experts on child development, has said, "We don't care for children because we love them; we love them because we care for them."

I realize this sounds kind of backward. And I'm not saying that the only reason we love our children is because we go through the motions of care. But for those times when biology isn't enough, it's good to have a backup. And that's exactly what many religious rituals surrounding children's early years provide. They make parents provide care, often in very public ways, and in so doing, they psychologically nudge parents' minds toward increased feelings of commitment to their children.

It might seem strange to say that parents need help staying committed to their children, but it makes sense. The parent-infant relationship is among the most one-sided of all human bonds. Parents must make huge sacrifices of time, money, and energy for little or no short-term gain. From the parents' point of view, it's all give and no take. For them, the benefits—having someone to help and support you emotionally, physically, and financially—only start accruing years later. In most areas of life, we humans prefer immediate satisfaction over delayed rewards, even when those delayed benefits are bigger. It's one reason so many of us spend more than we save, eat more than we should, or seek out other pleasures that can only harm us in the long term (e.g., any drug from nicotine to methamphetamine). When it comes to babies, we're built to get pleasure from coos, smiles, and snuggles as a way to offset these short-term costs. But sometimes those fleeting pleasures aren't enough.

Fortunately, the brain has a mental glitch of sorts that works to combat our desire for immediate pleasure. Psychologists call it the sunk cost fallacy. It's the idea that after having put money or other resources toward a goal, people become more likely to stick with that goal even if, objectively speaking, it no longer seems to be the most desirable option. It's why people who have paid to take a class or pursue a degree keep paying more to finish the program even if they don't like it. It's also why gamblers so frequently throw good money after bad. They feel their previous costs would be wasted if they stopped. But it's often more logical to cut your losses than to keep spending to justify what you started.

It's a bias that affects social relationships too. People often stay in poor ones because they feel they have already invested so much time and effort that it would be a shame to leave. So in many cases the sunk cost fallacy leads to irrational behavior.

Children aren't exactly a sunk cost. But, as I noted, the benefits they offer lag far behind the costs to time, energy, and money that parents incur. As a result, those expenditures—the ones made during the preceding days, weeks, and even years before children can "pay back"—can feel like sunk costs. If you're a parent, you may not think your mind is keeping track of these sacrifices, but it is subconsciously.

The good news is that, when it comes to children, this mental glitch can actually be an advantage. Your mind's resistance to forfeiting sunk costs counteracts its desire for immediate gratification. And in cases where the rewards for sacrifice are real but delayed—cases like parenting—that can be quite helpful and rational.

Rituals reinforce this advantage in three ways. The first is by increasing the feelings of sunk costs. Spending time, money, and effort to organize and host several ceremonies along with the gifts and other accessories they entail amounts to a sizable cost. Secondly, ceremonies enhance memory. Your brain will only use feelings of sunk costs to increase commitment to the extent that it encodes and remembers them. And while memories of the caretaking behaviors of the daily grind might grow dim, memories of major celebrations won't. The third and most important way rituals reinforce commitment is through their very public nature. Decades of psychological research show that we all cling harder to views and behaviors that we publicly announce or demonstrate. By taking part in several Shinto ceremonies designed to honor their children, Japanese parents publicly affirm and reinforce their devotion time and again. With each iteration, their minds' desire for consistency between acts and beliefs nudges those beliefs about their children's value to greater heights.

There's evidence to support this thesis that the repeated Shinto rituals we've seen here strengthen the bonds between parents and children. On average, the bond between Japanese mothers and their children is one of the most empathic and intimate of any culture. Note that I'm focusing on the mother-infant bond here, as across most cultures mothers tend to be the primary caretakers of children. This is especially evident in Japan, a country with one of the most gender-biased work cultures in the world. By custom, Japanese men are devoted to their employers. For most, this results in long hours spent away from the home. This gender bias can certainly cause much unfair stress for many Japanese mothers, who could otherwise pursue their careers as well.

Infancy

Still, when it comes to the mother-infant bond, Japanese mothers do everything they can to deepen it, even when controlling for their levels of available time. For example, they choose to spend more time near their children, engage in greater co-sleeping (this statistic includes fathers as well), have more skin-to-skin contact through play and bathing (again, this applies to Japanese fathers too), speak in warmer and more emotionally laden tones, and generally share more activities with their children than do most people in other cultures. These behaviors forge very deep bonds between mother and child—so much so that Japanese children tend to show less demanding and defiant behaviors when spending time with their moms than do children of many other nationalities.

In fact, the bond between Japanese mother and child is so strong and central to the culture that it produces a rather distinct emotion known as *amae*. Although the word *amae* has no direct translation into English, it can be described as a sense of intense closeness between mother and child—one where the child is feeling loved and cared for and the mother is enjoying cherishing her child. As an example, *amae* is the feeling that emerges when a young child climbs up on the lap of their busy mother, asking her to read a story, and she lovingly assents. It's that cherishing feeling that leads her to enjoy putting her child's needs first. Here, the child feels a comforting sense of being taken care of, and the mother feels a warm sense of being needed and trusted. That complex bundle of emotions—experienced in many different situations—is *amae*.

You don't have to be Japanese to feel *amae*; most parents have experienced something similar at times while raising their children. But the reason *amae* doesn't have a matching counterpart in English or many other languages is because it's not as common an experience as it is in Japan. Cultures develop labels for the emotions that they experience most frequently. And while states like sadness and anger are fairly common across the globe, others, like *amae*, only occur with regularity in certain places.

There's no way to prove conclusively that the Shinto rituals directly helped to create and reinforce Japanese parent-child bonds. To test this idea in a truly scientific way, we'd have to randomly select hundreds of nonreligious couples about to become pregnant, convert half of them to Shinto, ensure they perform these rituals, and then examine and compare the bonds they have with their children over the next seven years. For obvious ethical and practical reasons, that's an impossible experiment to carry out.

Still, I believe these rituals do play a central role in strengthening bonds. If I brought parents to my lab and had them repeatedly spend time and money to celebrate their child, I'd fully expect, based on a large body of scientific work, that their feelings and behaviors toward them would become even more positive afterward. From everything scientists know, these types of behaviors increase feelings of commitment and attachment.

Conducting these rituals not in a lab but in a more meaningful and public way that evokes even stronger emotions can only amplify the effects the rituals have on parental care and devotion, one that accumulates over time—a snowball effect. How parents feel and act toward their children on one day builds on all the feelings and actions that preceded that day. The more they act in ways that show care and devotion to their child, the more committed they become to keep doing so. And the more they remember such acts, spend time and money on them, and reflect on them, the better. There will always be bumps—events that can stress these bonds— but here again is why a series of rituals can help ensure parents don't metaphorically throw in the towel. You can think of these as booster shots for devotion. They can even leverage biology. As they nudge parents to increase or at least maintain caretaking, those actions in turn release more oxytocin to help cement the bonding.

You can already see some evidence for this idea—that simply acting out caring behaviors can create feelings of love—intuited in the recommendations that many physicians and parenting organizations offer to help people bond with their babies. Most recommend performing *rituals* (their word, not mine) that include regular times to massage the baby, to read them a story, to rock them while humming or singing. A time when the baby is the only focus. Such rituals, for all the reasons we've just seen, will further convince the mind that love for a child should and must be there, and, as a result, love *will* grow.

From the naming ceremony onward (or even before birth, as in Shinto), religious rituals offer tools to do just this. But you don't have to be a person of faith to benefit. In fact, if you go back and look at many of the Shinto practices I described, most aren't deeply religious in nature. Shinto prayers play only a small part. The main activities of almost all the ceremonies could be done in a completely secular way. What matters most in all cases is the ritualized repetition of the acts that makes them feel more special, meaningful, and public than eating a simple meal or giving a simple gift. By holding several ceremonies for your child during the first years of life, when their ability to give back is limited—maybe by adding quarter- or half-birthday celebrations, or celebrations with extended family focused on honoring different milestones in your child's development during the first years—you will deepen your feelings of connection. Even setting aside special times every day for activities that show devotion to a child—reading to, massaging, or playing a game—can help increase love and patience for them. Those feelings will prod you to keep the bonds between you strong and support you during the challenges that will invariably arise.

Parting the Clouds

In virtually every society, mothers bear the brunt of the challenges child-rearing entails. For this reason, many faiths have long recognized the need to give new mothers some sort of respite. In the month or two after birth, many religions have rituals and practices that relieve mothers of some or most of their new responsibilities. For example, Muslim mothers are encouraged to rest for up to forty days, during which they're exempted from many responsibilities. They don't need to complete certain prayers or religious obligations. Other people help with household chores. The I Ching, China's earliest book of divination, dictates that women should practice *zuo yue zi*, or "taking the month" as it's now colloquially called, to rest, eat, and sleep, without being disturbed by the normal intrusions of daily life. Hindu tradition, guided by Ayurvedic medical knowledge, also advocates that mothers spend a month or so being attended to by family so that they can rest and bond with their newborns, often with both benefiting from daily ritualistic massage.

Although these practices might simply seem like well-deserved pampering, they're an important backstop of sorts. As joyous as it can be to welcome a new child, it's also very stressful. Sleep and work routines change. Responsibilities intensify. And a crying infant regularly makes its needs known. For many, this stress is temporary; any uptick in anxiety or "baby blues" quickly dissipates. But for some mothers, those baby blues mark the start of a dangerous downward spiral to depression. And women who have suffered from depression earlier in life are at an even greater risk of experiencing it again during or after pregnancy.

On average, about 12 percent of new mothers will develop postpartum depression (PPD)—a figure that rises to 17 percent if we include cases where the depression began during pregnancy rather than after birth. Fathers, too, can experience depression following the birth of a child; the best estimates suggest that about 8 percent do.

For mothers, three broad factors tend to predict whether PPD develops. The first is how much anxiety a mother feels during her pregnancy, with chronic worry making PPD more likely. The second is a lack of social support. As you might imagine, the more support a new mother has in the period following birth, the more protected she will be against PPD. The third is stress. Living a more stressful life, whether due to uncertainties about economic or physical safety, increases the likelihood that a new mom will develop PPD.

The potential damage of PPD isn't limited to the mother. Its severity is linked to poorer outcomes for children, too, both immediate ones, including impaired bonding with parents, and long-term ones, such as increased behavioral problems and reduced cognitive abilities. As a result, PPD is particularly pernicious. It can lead mothers to feel guiltier because of the effect that PPD has on their children—and this guilt often intensifies depression.

Because of the threat posed by PPD, several faith traditions have developed tools to support new mothers. Through practices like *zuo yue zi* and, as we'll soon see, prayers of acceptance, religions have found ways to reduce anxiety and stress to combat PPD.

In the case of *zuo yue zi* and related traditions, it's important to recognize that how well these rituals work does depend on a few factors. Unlike the rituals that celebrate a baby's arrival—rituals that everyone looks upon with joy—these postpartum practices can be double-edged swords. It all depends on context. Anthropologists bundle all these rituals under the label "postpartum confinement." Almost all involve removing new mothers from their normal routines, usually by separating them from men or visitors in order to be cared for in relative privacy by their own mothers, mothers-in-law, or other female relatives. But whether such confinement feels like a luxury or a prison can vary.

Not every new mother relishes this change. And during the past several decades, with many societies across the globe in rapid economic and social transition, traditional roles are being upended at a faster rate, making it even more likely that many women might not see a value in adhering to these traditional rituals. Even though they may ultimately accept the practice due to family pressure, they might well feel that taking a monthlong respite would adversely affect their professional or social lives.

If, however, a new mother would like the respite and feels comfortable with those providing it, these rituals can offer a sizable psychological benefit. For example, in one study of 186 Taiwanese women, those who freely chose to follow the ritual practice of "doing the month" suffered from significantly fewer depressive symptoms. Similar findings come from a study on postpregnancy well-being among women in Hong Kong.

Religions have other ways to build support besides isolation periods. Just taking part in the regular activities of faith can be a great help. In fact, participating in religious activities even a few times per month decreases the likelihood of postpartum depression by more than 80 percent. It's well-known that getting support from a community of friends—help with chores, times to laugh or bond in a safe environment—protects against PPD. What's fascinating, though, is that being more religiously active increases this type of support for parents.

One way to see this comes from the puzzling finding that among religious families increasing numbers of children don't correspond to less quality time being spent with them or poorer long-term outcomes (e.g., education, wealth, health). Usually, as the number of children in a family grows, each child gets fewer resources. But this doesn't hold among those who are very religious, at least when compared to those who are completely secular.

One reason why is alloparenting. In the strictest sense, "alloparenting" means giving care to a child much as a parent would even though those children aren't direct descendants. So, if an aunt or a friend provides care for a child that usually falls to a mother or father, that aunt or friend is acting as an alloparent. And, of course, the more alloparenting that goes on in any one family, the more time the parents have to devote energy and resources toward things that benefit each of their children—more time to teach or care for them individually, or even to attend to other responsibilities that improve the family's, and thus each child's, opportunities.

In 2020, a groundbreaking study of over twelve thousand people confirmed that religious people are more likely to have a child than are those who identify as secular. More notably, it showed that as parents' involvement with their religion increases, so, too, does their ability to successfully raise more children. A central reason why was that stronger faith and stronger participation also increased the amount of alloparenting from community members who didn't have children of their own. By so doing, community members not only help parents increase the time and resources they can give to each of their children, they also help reduce the stress, anxiety, and guilt often felt by parents who are pushed to the limit.

As important as community support is for a new parent's well-being, belief can play a role as well. Since the brain is a prediction machine, it's always running simulations—what-ifs, if you will—as a way to help us prepare for what might be coming down the pike. When it comes to pregnancy and new children, those what-ifs can feel especially urgent: What if the baby isn't healthy? What if there's not enough money to take care of it? What if . . . ? You get the picture. Since heightened anxiety can make it more likely that women will have to deal with PPD or related types of psychological distress, anything that calms worry should help. And here's where a belief in God comes in.

The psychologist Andrea Clements has long studied religious surrender, which she defines as an active, intentional subordination of one's hopes and actions to God's will. This doesn't mean living in passive ignorance, simply expecting God to assist or punish you as It sees fit. But it does mean accepting that not everything is under your control and taking comfort in the fact that greater forces are shaping your destiny.

As Clements has found, religious surrender is an effective buffer against stress and anxiety. Those who accept this notion are calmer than the rest of us, both generally and in the face of specific anxiety-provoking events—like the ones that often occur around a baby's birth. Pregnant women who embrace a greater surrender as part of their religious beliefs and prayers experience less worry and stress during this time as well as lower rates of PPD at six months after their children are born. Similarly, women who report finding greater strength, comfort, and peace from their faith and prayers—a notion closely aligned with religious surrender—also experience PPD at much lower rates months after giving birth.

The upshot here is clear. Belief soothes worry. Avoiding the impulse to assess every possible outcome—many of which we can't control—eases stress, making us calmer and healthier.

These rituals suggest that whether or not we belong to a particular faith, we can make use of the tools faith has devised to handle what is arguably the greatest transition—birth—for both parents and newborns. Perhaps the easiest to apply outside of any particular religious tradition is isolating the new mother—as long as she welcomes the isolation and the people who will be helping her acclimate to the challenges of her new role. Many families already do something along these lines by having a dear relative or friend visit the family in the days or weeks after the new baby arrives.

I'd urge the families of any parent-to-be to find out what they need and to make time for them to rest and feel supported. It needn't be 24/7, although the more time, the better. What is essential, though, is doing it in a way that's special, preplanned, and orderly. I'm talking about a sort of care that's more formal than a friend dropping off supplies or stopping by to visit the parents for an hour. There's nothing wrong with such casual assistance, but it lacks the power that a more structured approach gives the new parents. The latter reduces their anxiety by bolstering their confidence in a network of friends and family whom they can always count on.

Belief in a deity also reduces anxiety, but even nonbelievers can access some of the benefits of psychological surrender we saw earlier. This may well be a trickier process in cognitive terms than establishing a support network, but it's possible. One needn't be a Buddhist to see the wisdom of the eighth-century Buddhist teacher Shantideva: "If a problem can be solved, what reason is there to be upset? If there is no possible solution, what use is there being sad?" Again, it may be tricky to adopt such a Zen stance right away, but its logic is undeniable and worth embracing. The idea is that surrender or acceptance can be given not only to God but also to fate or the inscrutable mechanisms of an extremely complicated universe. That probably won't make it any easier to deal with tragedy or misfortune if they do come, but it will free worrying minds from running every possible scenario beforehand and the stress that mindset always brings. Mindfulness means living in the present moment while not clinging to, yearning for, or dreading possibilities that may or may not ever come.

As we've seen, then, the primary challenge for children during the first few years of life is ensuring they get the care from family that they need to survive. This requires strengthening not only the commitment of their parents but also their parents' well-being. It's hard to care for someone if you're feeling distressed yourself.

Once children reach school age, though, their success will begin to depend more on others. How they behave will start to drive how the community views them. And with that change comes the possibility that selfish or unethical behaviors can harm their standing in the community—a harm that often has lasting effects. We humans are built to be social. We need the cooperation and company of others to thrive. Virtually all faiths take this into account by wielding spiritual technologies that build children's character and make them good citizens of their community, as we'll see in the next chapter.

2

The Formative Years: Learning What's Right and Wrong

A s children reach school age, those in families of faith also begin their immersion into the rituals and practices that will guide many of them through their whole lives. So we'll use that milestone as our opportunity to examine how these rites affect all believers. And, as we'll see, children are especially susceptible to their power.

Almost all faiths emphasize moral teachings. Many of their "textbooks" on the subject are familiar. Judaism and Christianity share the Ten Commandments. Buddhism has its Noble Eightfold Path. Islam has the ethics-laden Koran and Hadith. And while each of these contain guidelines unique to its own religion—what to eat, how to bathe, etc.—a common focus on character unites them all.

Of course, religion isn't the only way people learn to behave ethically. And we must acknowledge that there are many ethical atheists and unethical believers. But we must also acknowledge that religion is one of the oldest, and among the most effective, means of encouraging good behavior, particularly in large, complex communities of the sort that have dominated human civilization for the past six thousand years.

One way to see this is to compare the so-called big gods of the major world faiths to those that are more common in smaller communities. Big gods, like those of Christianity, Judaism, and Islam, tend to be omniscient, moralizing, and somewhat punitive. They know if you've sinned. They also know if you've repented, meaning if you haven't, there will be a supernatural price to pay. Hinduism and Buddhism don't have the same type of all-powerful single deity, or any deity at all in most forms of Buddhism, but have a similar concept: karma. Like big gods, the karmic calculator is all-knowing and keeps track of every transgression.

In comparison to these big gods of the world's major religions, the gods of smaller societies tend to be more transactional in nature and less moralistic in tone. If you need them to help you in some way, you make a prescribed offering. Interactions with them tend to be more of a give-and-take. These deities have practical power but usually less moral authority, and they hold little or no sway over whether or not you get into paradise.

Many anthropologists and psychologists believe that these different conceptions of the divine exist for a good reason: to combat dishonesty. For much of human history, our ancestors lived in small social groups, meaning that if someone was dishonest or unreliable, word would get around quickly, and they'd be ostracized. But as societies grew and relationships based on cooperation became more complex, dishonesty became easier to hide. If you were one worker out of hundreds on a project, coasting on others' efforts a little here and there wouldn't be that noticeable. If you were a scribe, falsifying financial records without getting caught would be fairly easy. Even today, if you want to bilk people out of their savings with an online scheme or cheat on your spouse with an online dating platform, urbanization and technology make such bad behavior all too easy to get away with. The anonymity of the individual in large societies makes cheating much more rampant, unless there's a check. And one great check is an all-knowing god who values virtue and punishes wrongdoers.

A review of cross-cultural and archeological findings supports this idea. If we rank societies by complexity, from small village communities, to large chiefdoms, to nation states, we find a corresponding increase in the percentage of religions based on big gods—from about 8 percent for small communities to 55 percent for large states. Likewise, the archeological record shows that the emergence of big-god religions tended to slightly precede the rise of more complex societies. The argument here is that larger societies—the ones where anonymous cheating is easier but cooperation is required—grew precisely because a check was placed on the dishonesty that might otherwise arise.

Perhaps the best evidence for this view comes from work by the anthropologist Joseph Henrich and colleagues, who asked more than five hundred people from many different cultures and religions to play a game in which they could anonymously cheat each other out of money. Henrich and his colleagues found that as people's belief in a god who punishes moral transgressions grew, so did their fairness. That is, those who believed in an omniscient, moralistic god were much less likely to cheat people from their own region or religion, and to share money more equally with them, than were those who believed in a less moralistic deity.

So believing that God wants you to behave virtuously helps you to be a good partner, friend, and citizen, with all the practical benefits that accrue from that goodness. And if enough people embrace virtue, their society functions more smoothly. Forming these be-liefs and behaviors early in life is an important step—so important that in cultures characterized by big gods, many children as young as six already believe that God knows about their sins.

Learning what God wants, and learning to care about it, differs from other types of learning. For one thing, you can't learn directly from God. You have to rely on intermediaries. For another thing, you can't see God's reactions to your actions. While it's easy for kids to know when their parents are angry or disappointed with them, that's not true of God. So religions rely on different technol-ogies both to help people learn what God expects from them and to live up to those expectations. Let's examine each in turn.

The Word of God

Five times a day, Muslims turn toward the Kaaba—one of Islam's holiest sites—in the city of Mecca to pray. These prayers—known as *salah*—have been recited in much the same manner for centu-ries, with the faithful bowing, kneeling, and touching their heads to the floor in a ritualized way as they praise God and ask for His guidance.

For many Jews, prayer happens three times a day, especially among members of Orthodox communities. Shacharit is the morn-ing service, then Mincha in the afternoon, and Maariv in the eve-ning (though the latter two are often combined near sunset, with Mincha taking place right before the sun drops below the horizon and Maariv right after). As in Islam, the emphasis in each ritual is on proclaiming God's glory and asking for His help and mercy.

Prayers like these are common among followers of many faiths. On a theological level, prayer makes great sense; it recognizes the deity's glory and asks for God's protection. But praying also works as a technology. How it's done matters a great deal. When people pray in a ritualized way—whether together or alone—their religion prescribes not only the words they say, but also how they say them. The cadence. The body movements. The direction of gaze. All these, as we'll see, have an effect.

While the power of prayer and learning the rules of a religion can reinforce people's belief and compliance at any age, it makes sense to begin that education early because young minds are the most malleable. That's why formal prayers are first taught to children quite early in life. Islam, for example, mandates that children start learning *salah* by seven years of age. Christian and Jewish children often begin their religious education even earlier by attending Sunday or Hebrew school.

Who leads those services and guides that education is important. Both are typically led by experts in the religion—priests, ministers, rabbis, imams, or their selected agents. That aura of expertise is important, as the minds of young children, much more so than adults, are naturally primed to seek wisdom from experts.

By four years of age, kids place more weight on a person's expertise than in how much they like them when deciding whether or not to accept new information they offer. In cases where a stranger seems to know what they're talking about more so than does a child's favorite teacher or friend, experiments show that kids as young as five are more willing to believe what the stranger says. When you combine this fact with research showing that kids better remember the same information when it comes from someone they see as credible, it quickly becomes clear that, for children, expertise trumps affection in deciding whom to believe. By extension, the word of a priest or rabbi holds more weight for most kids about what God wants them to believe or do than does that of a friend or even a parent.

One way religious leaders prove their expertise is through what's termed credibility-enhancing displays (CREDs). CREDs, which include demanding behaviors like fasting, sexual abstinence, and performing intricate rituals, aren't easy or enjoyable to do. And it's precisely because these behaviors are difficult that, when people choose to do them, they must have a good reason. In the case of religion, the reason for CREDs is a simple one: God desires them. So taking part in these difficult and demanding acts marks one as knowledgeable about and favored by God. And as a result, the words of religious leaders—the knowledge in the prayers they teach and the rules they dictate—tend to be embraced, especially by children's minds, as gospel.

Still, expertise and credibility matter in many domains. Scientists offer information about the world that we might not otherwise have. Mechanics offer information about our cars that we might not want. Yet somehow many of the things people learn within the context of religion seem more sticky. People tend to accept them more deeply, making any subsequent questioning of them, if it does occur, come with a greater sense of unease.

This brings me back to the power of the ways people pray. From a psychological perspective, it's a perfect storm for persuasion—one that goes way beyond simply being led or instructed by an expert.

When people say formal prayers—reciting the Our Father in Catholicism or the daily prayers of Islam and Judaism—the faithful come to know what God wants them to believe and how He wants them to behave. But, just for a moment, think about *how* people pray and listen—the actions of it. People say phrases over and over, kneel or bow, and sing or speak together. These ritualized acts bring a host of processes to bear on the mind that's not a random grouping of elements; it's too perfect to be.

To see why I say this, let's start with the notion of repetition. A good deal of research confirms that repeating statements, even false ones like "Elephants run faster than cheetahs," or "The population of North Dakota is larger than the population of New York State"—make them seem a bit more believable.

Psychologists now recognize that repeated exposure to ambiguous statements tends to increase people's belief in them—a phenomenon known as the illusory truth effect. For example, a recent study showed that even hearing a claim that seems difficult to accept (e.g., one that 80 percent of people believe is untrue) for a second time makes people give it a little bit more credence. It's not that they suddenly buy the information hook, line, and sinker. But people weren't quite as quick to reject it after the second go-round. As you might expect, repetition's effect on beliefs also holds true for children.

This illusory truth bias happens because the brain uses the ease with which we can retrieve something from memory as an indication of its likelihood. If you've seen or experienced something before, it's easier to recognize, and thus seems more likely to be true or to happen again. And the more times you see or hear it, the truer it rings. Imagine, then, the power that daily or weekly recitations of creeds and prayers can have on belief.

Repeating prayers and creeds doesn't only reinforce belief by affecting memory, however. As Jews recite the Shema, Christians the Apostles' Creed, or Muslims the *Shahada*—creeds expressing central tenets of their faiths—they're explicitly stating their belief in God and His commandments. From the brain's perspective, there's no reason, unless you're actively trying to deceive someone, to say something that you don't believe to some degree. You'd be even less likely to say such things in front of others if you thought they were false. Doing so—publicly stating something you might not fully believe—produces a state psychologists call cognitive dissonance, which is another powerful source of persuasion.

The theory of cognitive dissonance owes some of its origins and early tests to the study of a religion centered on extraterrestrials. In 1954, a small cult group led by Dorothy Martin, a homemaker in the Chicago suburb of Oak Park, believed that aliens were coming to save them from natural disasters that could end life on earth. So before gathering on Cuyler Avenue that Christmas Eve to sing carols while waiting to be saved, they had faithfully removed all metal from their bodies—a precaution Ms. Martin, who they believed communed with aliens from the planet Clarion, told them was necessary to safely enter the aliens' saucers. But perhaps what was most interesting about this event was that it wasn't the first time many of these people had placed their hope in Ms. Martin's messages only to be let down; it was the fourth. So strong was the group's belief that it not only led many to leave their jobs or spouses behind to await their alien saviors, but also to hold fast to their beliefs time and again in the face of contradictory evidence.

Unbeknownst to the cult members, a few social psychologists infiltrated their ranks in an attempt to understand why their beliefs were so resolute. What the psychologists found confirmed a basic tenet of their emerging theory: people feel uncomfortable when their beliefs and their behaviors don't match, and so they're very motivated to resolve the inconsistency. Unless you're an actor onstage, believing one thing but behaving in a way that contradicts it makes you feel stress. To dispel that stress, you can do one of two things: change your behaviors to match your beliefs, or change your beliefs to match your behaviors. But in the case of public behaviors that you can't easily take back, like proselytizing the end of the world due to extraterrestrials, giving up beliefs can become quite difficult. And so people find ways to protect them.

One lesson of cognitive dissonance theory, which has been supported by vast amounts of evidence over decades, is that the first way to resolve tension is easy. If, for example, you believe you're an honest person but just told a lie, apologize and never tell a lie again. It'll be easy for you to go back to feeling like you're an honest person if you just change your behavior. Likewise, if you don't believe in God but just recited a prayer attesting that you do, stop going to church and reciting that prayer. But changes like these aren't always easy to make, especially if you're a child whose parents are taking you to church or temple. So if you can't change your behavior to match your beliefs—if you can't easily stop attending religious services and reciting prayers to a God you're not sure exists—you're left with a second and often more psychologically challenging option: you can change your beliefs to match your behavior.

Numerous experiments have proven that people's beliefs gradually change to match the words they say. This doesn't happen if someone forces or strongly entices you to say something that contradicts your position. In those cases, it's easy to discount your dissonant acts. But if you say something repeatedly in a situation where you seem to be doing it of your own choosing or with only mild encouragement, your beliefs will begin to shift. And this is especially true for beliefs that aren't strongly held. So imagine a child, whose beliefs about God aren't well-defined, professing the tenets of the faith in front of adults and peers at weekly services. I guarantee you that they'll internalize those beliefs more and more as time progresses.

When it comes to learning what God wants via prayer and worship, there's one other element to consider: what people do with their bodies. Across many religions, praying is accompanied by similar bodily movements like bowing and kneeling that suggest a type of reverence and deference. Some religions also use rhythmic motions. Jews, for example, often sway forward and back while saying prayers—a practice known as "shuckling."

Movement matters because your brain is constantly keeping track of your body's positions in space. It's one reason why you can walk, sit down, or stand up with your eyes closed. You don't fall over doing this because your brain doesn't need visual information to know where it is relative to the rest of your body, though it uses that information when it's available. Every moment you're alive your brain is constantly using feedback from throughout your body to generate predictions about where that body begins and ends.

The result is a phenomenon psychologists refer to as embodied thought—a term that implies thoughts are shaped not only by abstract ideas and memories but also by feedback from all the senses. For example, when you remember a piece of your favorite birthday cake, you can almost taste it as your salivary glands respond. When you recall riding a roller coaster, you can feel slight butterflies in your stomach as you imagine going over the peak. Those physical feelings influence how the brain encodes things—what features it most attends to and how it interprets incoming information—not only when that information is first encountered but also each time it's recalled.

When people lower their heads or bodies by bowing or kneeling, they take a position that the brain interprets as one of low power or status. I don't mean just symbolically; I mean that those positions actually make people feel less powerful relative to others. Ample studies have shown that our minds use vertical position as a cue to our rank relative to others. For example, experiments have shown that people routinely judge images of other people, objects, or animals to be more powerful when they're placed above other images of the same type. Likewise, if we take positions below others, we feel both lower in status and more concerned with garnering approval.

Perhaps most relevant for prayer, though, is the simple fact that gazing upward makes us more willing to accept and embrace advice and information. Remarkable evidence of this comes from an experiment in which people had to read purported facts and opinions on screens positioned at different heights. When they read information presented on screens placed above eye level, they were more than twice as likely to shift their views and accept that information. When we kneel to recite prayers to God—who in our mind's eye, occupies a position above us—we become more open to embracing the words of those prayers.

When people pray together, the power of synchrony comes into play too. Yes, people certainly pray by themselves, but there are also many times when they pray in communion with others— when Muslims bow and kneel in unison during *salah*, when the chanting and shuckling in Jewish synagogues synchronizes, or when Catholics stand and kneel together as they recite the prayers of Mass.

In the introduction, I explained how synchronous movement among people makes them feel more similar to one another. That plays as important a role for building beliefs as it does for building community. Decades of research have shown that we're more persuaded by people to whom we feel connected. Hearing this information in the presence of synchrony makes us remember it better and believe it more fully.

When you put all these different pieces together, the result is a forceful interplay of psychological levers that simultaneously enhance memory, manipulate cognitive dissonance, use body positions, and synchronize movements. All combined, it's an impressive technology that helps children and adults absorb and embrace the tenets of their faith. But while belief can guide behavior, sometimes a little nudging can help.

Nudging Virtue

The Catholic Mass, to which members of the faith flock every Sunday, is a highly ritualized event. The presiding priest stands on an elevated dais in robes adorned with religious symbols as he reads from scripture and gives a sermon. Worshippers recite a series of prayers during which they stand, bow their heads, and kneel in specific sequences in a hall that usually has a vaulted ceiling and stained-glass windows that cast softly colored patterns on the floors below. Music tends to echo through the nave as worshippers sing hymns together. For all the reasons I noted above, it would make good sense that attending Mass would reinforce people's faith. But there's another question to consider: Does taking part in the Mass also work to change people's behavior *in the moment*—ways that don't depend on the longer-term process of internalizing beliefs? If it does, we should be able to see some evidence that attending Mass nudges people toward virtue while they're there.

One initial piece of support comes from research by Duke Univeristy psychologist Patty Van Cappellen. Her team set out to see if attending Mass pushed people to suddenly be more charitable. By working with priests from twenty different Catholic parishes, Van Cappellen was able to ask more than five hundred parishioners to complete surveys right after they had just finished attending Sunday Mass. The surveys inquired about people's beliefs, their feelings of community with those around them, their emotional states, and what they would choose to do with a windfall of money if it came their way.

Since the people taking part in this study were already at Mass

(and regularly attended it), their faith was already fairly strong. Nonetheless, in that moment, Van Cappellen found that many people's sense of community and social connection to others was directly tied to taking part in the Mass rituals. And this sense of connection was itself directly linked to how much money they said they would give to others rather than keep for themselves. Put another way, those whose sense of community was most reinforced during the Mass were the ones who planned to act most virtuously by sharing their windfalls. In this way, you can see another route—one distinct from beliefs—by which weekly, or even daily, rituals push people to be less selfish.

Still, people's intentions don't always match their actions. A skeptic could easily suggest that just because people said they'd act less selfishly doesn't mean, when real money was on the line, that they'd actually do it. So proving that religious rituals make people more moral can benefit from a different tack—one where "sins" can actually be measured.

We can see the combined power that belief and prayer have on morality from an experiment where researchers gave people an opportunity to cheat on a test. To provide some incentive to cheat, the researchers promised a hundred dollars to whoever answered the most questions correctly. And because people completed the study in isolation while using computers with access to the internet, cheating was easy; Google was just a mouse click away. But, unbeknownst to the test takers, the researchers had a way to know who, if anyone, used it.

Now, here's where prayer comes in. Before they took the quiz, the researchers asked half the people to compose a prayer. The results were remarkable. On their own, neither being religious nor saying a prayer directly affected whether someone would cheat. But certain combinations of the two did. Among those who

believed in God, praying before taking the quiz made them more honest. But among those who didn't hold religious beliefs, saying a prayer, which obviously felt meaningless and inauthentic, actually increased cheating. It seems, then, that simply identifying as religious or espousing religious beliefs doesn't always make people more virtuous on its own. Sometimes they need the added ritualistic nudge to think about God's wishes that prayer provides in the moment.

In fact, when we look at the links between religion and ethical behavior, it's clear that daily and weekly practices do much to build and maintain character. If you lump all religious people together—combining the devout with others who aren't quite as devoted or engaged in their faiths—and compare them with atheists, there are no differences in their moral behavior. But if you use a finer-grained analysis—one that separates religious people by degree of engagement with the practices and rituals of their faith—a very different picture emerges. For example, Israelis who live in religious kibbutzim tend to behave more honestly and fairly than do those who live in secular ones. Likewise, more devout Muslims—those who study daily to become imams—also tend to act more ethically than their less religious peers.

Findings like these suggest that while religious beliefs can play a role in guiding ethical behavior, the more often people engage in the rituals meant to support these ideals, the better. Put another way, it's easy to forget or ignore what we're supposed to believe and do unless and until we're reminded. For instance, studies show Christians are more generous and watch less porn on Sundays after leaving services, but during the rest of the week they don't differ on these measures from more secular folks.

At its core, moral behavior requires self-control. It's natural to want to do what feels good in the here and now, but overindulging

in things that bring immediate pleasure—sex, eating, imbibing, spending, or even violence—usually leads to ruin in the long run.

Children younger than seven have a difficult time overcoming their selfish urges. But thereafter, as they begin to learn what other people expect from them, they can, often with reminders, develop their nobler sides. And those who develop better self-control are the ones who generally succeed the most in life.

Here's where the genius of religion again comes into play. As we just saw, taking part in the rituals and practices of a faith not only increases belief but also strengthens virtuous motives in the moment. In many Muslim communities, the call to prayer can be heard echoing through the streets multiple times per day. And it's at these exact times that Muslim shopkeepers are most generous. Research confirms that they'll give more to charitable requests made during or just after hearing the call than at other times. The sound of the call reminds them of what God and the community value, and their giving goes up.

Sometimes just being surrounded by divine symbols does the trick. Hindus who agreed to play a game where they could choose between taking smaller amounts of money from a common pool of cash—which meant that there would still be money in the pool for others—or larger amounts—which meant they'd gain at another's expense, were more likely to take less if they played while sitting in a temple than if they were sitting in a restaurant kitchen. Those in the kitchen took 36 percent more rupees out of the pool on average.

Even in day-to-day life, simple religious reminders—some that barely register in our consciousness for more than a second or two—can have a similar effect. A great example comes from an experiment in which people completed word puzzles, some of which contained religiously toned words (e.g., "divine," "spirit," "sacred") and some of which didn't. Afterward, the researchers gave people ten dollars and told them that they could keep as much of it as they would like. Any amount they left would be given to people in another study that didn't offer payment. Here again, a reminder of religion led to more generosity. People who had completed puzzles with religious words left more than twice as much money for others.

There are many other examples like these, but the conclusion is an obvious one: nudging the mind to focus, even for a second, on God or religious symbols pushes people toward virtue. Yet, the tools by which prayer and ritual have been designed to move the mind consist of even more basic elements—ones that can work even in the absence of belief in God. Ones that leverage some of the mind's most fundamental mechanisms, and ones that scientists have only truly begun to unlock in the past few decades: our emotions.

Among the many feelings we humans experience are some that possess a moral cast—gratitude, awe, elevation—that makes them especially appropriate to spiritual work. All emotions shape our expectations and behaviors. But these three in particular guide our moral perceptions and actions.

The links between these emotions and religion emerge quite early in life. Beginning around age four, children associate prayer with positive feelings, especially gratitude. As the difficulties of life mount with age, they come to recognize that prayer can also help with problems and negative feelings. But even so, prayer remains a way for everyone to boost positive emotions like gratitude, awe, and elevation (a type of intense admiration). To see exactly how these emotions can influence our moral behavior, let's take a look at each in turn.

Gratitude

Teens cite feeling grateful as one of their four most popular reasons for embracing religion. If you believe that God or the universe is generous, it makes complete sense to feel a strong, persistent sense of appreciation. But the relationship between gratitude and belief in God works the other way too. For example, research shows that people who were randomly assigned to pray for others over a four-week period felt more intense gratitude in their daily lives than did those who were assigned simply to think about other people in a positive way.

Feeling grateful doesn't only increase belief in God; worshipping God also increases gratitude. And when it comes to reinforcing morality, that second part truly matters, as gratitude boosts self-control. In my own research, I've found that when people feel grateful, they're much less likely to succumb to temptations for immediate gratification that often lead them to be impulsive and selfish. I also find that making people feel grateful, either by having them count their blessings or through a staged event where an actor helps them solve a problem, causes them to cheat others less and help others more, even when these others are complete strangers. As long as those feelings of gratitude last, people behave in more prosocial ways. So when you offer thanks to God—saying grace or similar blessings before meals, reciting formal prayers of thanksgiving at services, or even lighting candles or giving small offerings as a sign of appreciation to deities—the gratitude you feel is already pushing you to be more moral.

Awe

This emotion is best characterized by feelings of wonder in facing something vast, great, or even incomprehensible. Awe works much like gratitude does to promote virtue. For example, experiments show that when people are made to feel awe, such as by showing them scenes of vast canyons, towering mountains, and sweeping plains, they subsequently report greater belief in God's existence and control of the natural world. Other research shows that awe, like gratitude, increases generosity, honesty, and feelings of connection.

Now, it's certainly true that awe tends to be experienced less frequently in daily life than gratitude. Yet it's also true that most religions provide opportunities to feel it. One way is through having people listen to stories and sermons about God's powers. Another, subtler way is through architecture.

Sacred spaces—those where prayer and rituals often take place—tend to emphasize both beauty and a sense of vastness in which worshippers feel relatively small. A glance at iconic cathedrals, mosques, and temples throughout the world will quickly illustrate the point. These venues are adorned with artistic details that add to their beauty as well as soaring ceilings—heights that evoke the heavens.

Smaller houses of worship also do their best to convey awe. Even more secular spaces designed for contemplation often make use of these themes through incorporating architectural features that use or reflect elements of the natural world—sunlight, beautiful views, cave-like enclosures. What's common to all these spaces is an attempt to evoke awe in those who enter. So, as you sit in a pew, kneel in a mosque, or worship in a temple, simply viewing the space around you makes feelings of awe more likely. And those feelings, experienced regularly, strengthen belief, community, and virtue.

Elevation

Elevation is what we feel when we see someone perform an extraordinary act of moral goodness. It's characterized by sensations of warmth and expansion in the chest, along with admiration and affection for the person who does the extraordinary thing. Stories of gods, of historical or modern-day saints, benevolent leaders, and even social activists can also make us feel elevation. Celebrity isn't necessary, though. Witnessing any noble act, even one by a nameless stranger, can also do the trick.

Like gratitude and awe, elevation works to reinforce people's kindness and support for one another. And religious texts are an especially rich repository of elevation-inducing tales. Research has confirmed that reading or hearing such stories causes people to feel elevation—a feeling that motivates them to help others. And the more often people experience elevation, the more automatic the feeling becomes. It's as if hearing these noble stories creates a habit of mind, a predisposition to behave virtuously that, in turn, evokes elevation in other people, nudging them to do the same.

Although the internet and the nightly news offer their fair share of elevating tales, for many people, the most common place to hear stories about human virtue is in houses of worship and religious education classes. It's there that children regularly learn about the lives of the saints, patriarchs, and martyrs. And it's there that the habit of elevation typically first begins.

To my mind, much of the power religion holds for building character comes from nudges like these that target our emotions, our feelings of connection, and our attachments to beliefs. Throughout this chapter, I've kept using the term "nudge" intentionally. While its colloquial meaning is familiar, it also has a technical meaning in the behavioral sciences. As Richard Thaler and Cass Sunstein describe it, a nudge is anything that through a relatively small and efficient mechanism can alter people's behaviors in predictable ways.

While much of the literature on nudges centers around economic or policy decisions, nudges can be useful for morality too. For example, when people who owe back taxes are told via instructions on a tax form that nine out of ten people pay their taxes on time and that they were in the minority who hadn't, they repay those debts at a much higher rate than other tax delinquents. Just one sentence can move the moral needle.

Nudges on tax forms are great, but they pale in comparison to the tactics religions use. Whereas government agencies, corporations, or health programs might employ single nudges to alter people's behavior, religious practices and rituals weave multiple nudges into a symphony composed of prayer, synchrony, repetition, feelings, and even posture.

What we as influencers—whether for social change or our own daily choices—should take from this is that we can up our game. Single nudges are great; multiple nudges are better. If we push, pull, and constrain the mind via several approaches at the same time, we'll magnify their effects.

Now, it's true that many of these religious nudges depend on people already holding certain beliefs. For example, nudges provided by prayer instill honesty only in people who already believe in God. This doesn't mean that using multiple-nudge strategies to enhance character requires belief in God. Gratitude, awe, and elevation can increase honesty, generosity, kindness, and other ethical behaviors in any context, including secular ones.

If you're a parent looking for ways to foster good character in your kids, create an environment that encourages these emotions. Show that it's okay to ask for help and important to show gratitude for it. Teach that taking time to enjoy the beauty of nature or to recognize the good in others is worthwhile. And most important, ritualize these activities. Make it a point to read an elevating story about someone at a set time every week. Set aside a time for milk and cookies when everyone talks about things that made them feel gratitude during the past week. And try to combine as many elements simultaneously as you can. For example, recite a favorite poem about kindness or gratitude together out loud. While the result might not be as finely tuned a package as many religions use, it will still help you shape your children's character while also nudging your own.

You can magnify the effect of these rituals by drawing in people beyond your family circle whenever you can. As I noted above, children usually start learning about what God and society expect of them via prayer and rituals when they are between five and seven years of age. By that point, the importance of feeling connection with their peers is growing as well. Rituals can foster morality by enhancing these bonds—bonds that will help foster character development through positive peer pressure and support.

Cristine Legare, a psychologist at the University of Texas at Austin, showed the remarkable power of rituals to foster community among kids in an ingenious experiment. She randomly divided a bunch of children taking part in an after-school program into two teams: green and yellow. So that it'd be easy to remember who was on which team, she had them wear green and yellow wristbands. Next, she divided each group in half again so that there were two green and two yellow groups, all with about the same number of boys and girls. For the next two weeks, she had one of the green and one of the yellow groups perform a ritual with beads for ten minutes a day while the other groups played with the beads however they liked.

The point here was to see whether taking part in simple rituals would increase the bonds between kids beyond simply dividing them into teams and letting them interact. During the ten-minute activities, the kids on the green and yellow teams in the ritual condition were told to string the beads in a very specific way. They first had to touch a star-shaped bead to their foreheads, then put the string through the bead. Next, they clapped their hands three times before getting a round bead and touching it to their heads. Then they began the sequence again, and on it went. The kids in the nonritual condition were told to string the beads any way they wished.

After two weeks, Legare asked the children questions to gauge how much they valued their peers. Given the human mind's tribal nature, all children showed a preference for kids in their own group. But the strength of this preference—the degree to which kids felt attached to the others wearing the same color—was much greater among those who had also performed the ritual together every day. In other words, they liked their teammates much more if they had performed rituals with them than if they hadn't.

You can easily incorporate rituals like these into many types of play activities, as Legare's work shows, or enhance their effect even further by combining them with singing songs or reading stories focused on moral themes. Doing so will lay the foundations of good character while forming the social bonds that reinforce it. It will also begin to prepare children for the next challenge of life: the transition to adulthood.

Coming of Age:
Adulting Isn't Easy

I n small villages nestled in the Amazon rain forest, elders of the Sateré-Mawé huddle around a stewing brew of cashew leaves and herbs. It's sickly green in color, has an oily consistency, and a smell that's been described as everything from acrid motor oil to a fetid puddle on the jungle floor. But for the twelve- and thirteen-year-old boys who are about to take part in the coming-of-age ritual called *waumat* for the first time, it's not the steaming concoction that evokes dread. It's the pulsating mass of *Paraponera clavata*, better known as bullet ants, that sits in a container nearby. They're called bullet ants because the pain of their sting rivals that caused by being shot—a pain thirty times worse than a bee sting. The worst part, though, is that the ordeal doesn't end quickly. The pain of the sting is usually accompanied by vomiting, shaking, and sometimes mild paralysis for up to twenty-four hours.

Before the rite begins, the tribal elders dunk the ants into an herbal brew. Not to agitate them, but to anesthetize them. The agitating part comes later, after the sleeping ants are handwoven into a pair of gloves made from leaves and palm fronds. When the ants wake up, they're angry and ready to attack whoever is wearing those gloves—a fact the young boys know all too well. During *waumat*, each boy must put on these gloves and face the pain as their first step to adulthood.

In preparation for the ceremony, the boys have been adhering to food taboos for days—forgoing some of the treats they usually like to consume. Their hands have also been adorned with symbols painted on with a black dye. One by one, each initiate places his hands into the ant-lined gloves, which themselves have been adorned with red macaw feathers to denote the sacrifices of war and white hawk-eagle feathers to symbolize the need for courage.

Almost immediately, the ants' stingers begin to pierce the wearer's skin, and the quickly intensifying pain can be seen on his face. But to the best of his ability, each boy tries to remain stoic, believing that showing no emotion—no fear or shying away from the suffering—marks him as a worthy member of the tribe. After the ceremony ends, the boys link arms to sing and dance late into the evening. Those linked arms serve two purposes: to show solidarity, but also to help hold each other up as the ant venom causes their leg muscles to spasm. By repeating *waumat*, sometimes as many as twenty times over a series of months, the boys come to be viewed by others in the tribe as worthy of the privileges and responsibilities of adulthood: being recognized by the *tuxaua* (village leader) as an independent voice, marrying, and even warring if necessary.

On the other side of the earth, groups of male Maasai adolescents rove the semi-arid lands of Kenya and Tanzania in preparation for their own coming-of-age rites. These travels, accompanied by elders of the tribe, are meant to announce the formation of an age-set and the coming rites of passage. For the Maasai, an age-set is pretty much what it sounds like: a permanent grouping of people near the same age who move together through the phases of life. Near the end of this prescribed period of travel, the local *oloiboni*, or prophet, will choose a location for the rite where the community will build a group of huts to house the participants and attendees.

For seven days before the rite of *emuratare*, which centers on circumcision, the initiates tend cattle herds to prove their prowess at this essential part of Maasai life. Then, on the night preceding *emuratare*, the boys sleep outside the village in the forest. At dawn, they race to the huts and enter, shouting like raiders intent on plundering the village. But rather than terrorize the villagers, they chant and dance almost nonstop throughout the day. Then, in turn, each douses himself with cold water and makes his way to the tent for the main event while being taunted that he won't be strong enough to make it through without screaming or crying.

Once he's ready, an elder skilled in the art slices off the foreskin of his penis. Throughout the process, the boy is expected to remain utterly silent. Any flinch would be a sign of shameful weakness. When the rite is over for everyone, the newly emerging men don black robes and paint their faces with white chalk—a mode of dress they will maintain for several months as they heal. When the end of the healing period finally comes, the entire community hosts a celebration where the new men receive their own cattle and are shown the respect that their new station in society brings.

Of course, rites of passage aren't only for boys. The transition through adolescence is just as pivotal for girls, and most religions have corresponding rites for them as well. When girls reach puberty, the Sateré-Mawé remove them from the village to a hut in the forest where they will live in isolation for two months, with only their mothers allowed to see them and bring them food. The Maasai, in a practice similar to what they do with males, subject teenage girls to female circumcision. Both of these, like the corresponding male rites, require the teens to stoically endure hardship and pain. But the female rites are less elaborate because of women's lower status in Maasai society.

Overall, the complexity of such rituals corresponds closely to the status that each gender holds within its culture. Among the Apache, a tribe where women's status is on par with men's, rites of passage for girls are both demanding and intricate. For the Apache, Changing Woman, or *Asdzáá Nádleehé*, is one of the most honored deities. She represents the powers of life, of fertility, and of the changing seasons. And as her name suggests, she is always in flux. She grows old in winter, but by spring she regains her youth. As such, she symbolizes the principal forces that undergird the rhythms of Apache life. And in *Na'ii'ees*, known in English as the Sunrise Ceremony, adolescent girls (the summer after their first menstruation) take on her form to channel those powers on their way to becoming adults.

The Sunrise Ceremony unfolds over a few days. Throughout the ceremony, many people dance. Some dance with bells around their legs that clang to the rhythm of the drums. Some have animal motifs painted on their bodies. But the primary event—the one that everyone has come to see—is the dance of the guest of honor: the girl who will become a woman.

This rite can take several forms, but the following details are common to most. In an open field at sunset, the girl, wearing a buckskin dress, appears, accompanied by drums and chanting. She puts salt in her mouth to protect her from evil. Her mother and godmother give her an eagle feather to impart strength and a piece of abalone shell, which is the symbol of Changing Woman. Next, the medicine man gives her a wooden cane that she must hold at all times and use in her dancing to strike the ground. Then the grueling ritual begins. She dances, bobbing and stepping up and down to the unceasing drumbeat. She cannot stop; she cannot rest, no matter the pain. It's not until after over thirty songs have been chanted, often taking almost the entire night, that she can finally sleep.

The next morning comes quickly, though. Before sunrise, everyone gathers in the field to witness the girl's transformation. Hours of dancing begin again. Yet this time she lies down at one point on a deerskin placed before her. As people recite prayers, the girl's godmother massages her to reduce the pain and prepare her for her next challenge.

As the drums rise, she must run across a field in the four cardinal directions, each representing one of the phases of life: infancy, childhood, adulthood, and old age. Her elders then dust the exhausted girl with pollen, the sign of fertility, so that her face becomes golden. In this moment, she becomes Changing Woman incarnate. Now she has the power to offer blessings and cures. But as she dances for several more hours, she must avoid falling or pausing. She must endure the pain that represents all of life's trials. And when her family finally washes the pollen away, she emerges from beneath it as a changed woman—one who has demonstrated her grit and her willingness to be a full-fledged member of her tribe.

Although the specifics of these three rites—*waumaut, emuratare*, and *na'ii'ees*—differ dramatically, they all start to move teens toward adulthood via the same deeply seated psychological mechanisms: one designed to prove maturity and competence, and one designed to prevent backsliding into the easier comforts of childhood.

Building an Adult

As we saw in the previous chapter, education isn't meant only to impart factual knowledge; it's also meant to shape the beliefs, connections, and social skills necessary to make one part of a community. But even when education works well, the changes in roles and responsibilities that accompany adolescence can evoke hesitation or outright resistance. Becoming mature means fending for yourself, and that's not always something you want when you've been ensconced in the comparative comforts of childhood. Nor is it always an easy transition for parents and community members to accept when, for years, they've grown used to caring for and guiding you.

Beyond the psychological uncertainty that complicates adolescence, there's a physiological uncertainty: the biological changes of puberty emerge over several years. Should we see adulthood commencing when voices change or menarche comes? Maybe. But I'm not sure it's wise to expect twelve- or thirteen-year-olds to start thinking and behaving like adults when their frontal cortices—the parts of the brain that control impulsivity and decision making—still have about a decade's worth of growth to go. Some cultures, like the Japanese, say adulthood begins at twenty. But in cultures with a lower life expectancy, an earlier start might be more practical.

Since the date at which adulthood arrives can't easily and universally be tied to a single psychological or bodily change, it makes figuring out when someone becomes an adult tricky. Still, it's useful for a community to have some consensus about when its members should start "adulting." Otherwise, some people might try to remain dependent long after they should have spread their wings, while others will chafe against the constraints placed upon their burgeoning sense of independence.

Coming of Age

I don't have the best answer for when adulthood should arrive. In fact, I don't believe there is a conclusive answer. But I can say that cultures around the world—some more definitively than others—have set different guidelines for when the process should begin. Guidelines that, at least historically, seemed to fit their needs. And here's where religious coming-of-age rites fill an important role.

All these rituals have two main goals. That's because moving successfully through adolescence entails meeting two challenges. First, an adolescent's family and community have to believe that a person who has changed little in the past few days or months suddenly possesses a slew of different qualities. Second, and sometimes even more challenging, the person undergoing the rite has to believe this fact themselves. The teen who yesterday relied on their parents for everything must today start accepting responsibility.

If you look across the globe, you'll find a mosaic of coming-of-age rites—ones where the participants' social roles are transformed using different combinations of pain, stoicism, erudition, perseverance, and posing, all under the approving eye of the divine. But if you take a closer look—if you peek at the mind's inner workings—you'll find that two psychological levers do most of the heavy lifting.

The first is self-control. To be a successful adult, you need to demonstrate competence and reliability. The former is essential to functioning on your own. The latter is necessary for people to believe that they can count on that competence—that they can count on you to do your part. From a psychological perspective, competence and reliability share one thing in common: people need self-control for both. It's what gives people the grit to persevere toward goals of knowledge and skill acquisition rather than throw in the towel. It's what makes them accept responsibilities rather than shirk them.

In fact, when we're deciding who's responsible, we place such a great emphasis on self-control that even when we're not actively thinking about whether other people have it, our brains are subtly keeping score. When we see people who show signals that they might be lazy or unreliable, even if only in specific situations, our minds automatically tag them as less trustworthy. So while the rituals I described in the last chapter were meant to help young people build self-control, the rituals here are meant to prove to others that they have it. Think of them as exams of sorts.

By itself, ritualistically displaying self-control can't produce enduring changes in anyone's social role. Self-control is a necessary but not sufficient mechanism for any rite of passage to work. That's why there's a second lever: self-fulfilling prophecies.

The term "self-fulfilling prophecy" was coined by the sociologist Robert K. Merton to signal that a belief or prediction, whether or not it's factually correct, could produce its expected outcome. Merton's classic example is that of a bank people believed to be going under. Whether or not this expectation was true for any given bank, people believing it would make a run on the institution to withdraw their money before the doors were locked. Any bank, even one with good financial standing, would be forced to close if all of its customers tried to withdraw their money at once. In this way, a prophecy of the bank's doom, even if untrue at the start, would bring about the predicted result.

Psychologists have found that the same phenomenon applies to people. If you expect certain things from them, you'll tend to act in ways that make it more likely that those things will emerge. A famous example can be seen in the Pygmalion effect—a finding that showed teachers' expectations for a child's academic success affected the students' subsequent performance. Because they expected certain kids to be more academically gifted, teachers gave them more attention and encouragement, thereby bringing the false prophecy of their academic superiority to fruition.

Self-fulfilling prophecies aren't limited to intelligence, though. Mothers' expectations of how much alcohol their teens will consume predict how much they actually will drink. The same goes for weight. If people expect another person to overeat (even if they don't), they'll put out more food, which leads to overeating. The impact of self-fulfilling prophecies is usually strongest when multiple people hold the same expectations for a person and when those expectations occur at the start of a new role—characteristics that accurately describe the situation surrounding rites of passage.

It makes sense, then, that rituals the world over aim to show that those entering adolescence have the self-control to begin to be treated as equals in the community, and to nudge those same community members to reinforce that view. In so doing, the simple act of expecting teens to behave more like adults increases their confidence and motivation to do so. Yet the exact ways in which religions go about these rites can differ a great deal. Historically, these rites often relied on tolerating pain and exhaustion to prove one's self-control. Today, some more traditional cultures retain that method, as we saw in the three rites of passage I described above. Cultures where adults' success depends less on meeting physical challenges have adopted other ways to prove self-control. To understand that evolution, let's trace the development of these tactics to see how they attempt to meet the challenges of changing times.

By Pain

Many religious traditions require young people to undergo a painful or physically exhausting ritual to demonstrate their mastery of self-control both to the community and to themselves.

To be a valued, independent member of most communities, you have to be strong and resilient. And enduring pain is one way to show it. Even scientists who study self-control often measure it by seeing how long people can tolerate pain, though not pain anywhere near the intensities found in the rites I described earlier. That type of pain isn't part of normal life. It's extreme. Stoically meeting these ritualized challenges is nothing short of exceptional.

These rites are especially transformative because they occur within the context of a period of shifting identity. For instance, Sateré-Mawé adolescent girls have been isolated in huts. Maasai male teens have been traveling and herding without family members. These changes, which have upended their sense of what's normal, prime them to become open to the extreme abnormality the rituals impose. As a result, the unusual, demanding, immersive acts at the core of these rituals have an easier time eroding the adolescents' sense of normality, making them more susceptible to the new normal that's now expected of them. This is a concept some readers might recognize from the rigors of military basic training, in which intense physical activity and deprivation are used to metaphorically knock people down in order to build them back up again. The effect isn't limited to the adolescents themselves. The rituals' intensity also changes the way onlookers see the initiates. It alters their sense of reality, making community members more open to embracing the altered status of the adults-to-be.

In the previous chapter, we examined the phenomenon of cognitive dissonance, and it applies here too. When teens act in ways that show self-control, any beliefs they had that they were still weak and immature would lead to a state of mental tension. And because you really can't undo an act or behavior like those in these rites, the easiest way to resolve the tension would be changing your belief. So imagine the Apache girl who has just completed the grueling requirements of the Sunrise Ceremony. Even if she doubted herself at the start, she now has ample proof of her own strength and resilience—a fact that must alter how she views her own abilities and maturity.

Another aspect of cognitive dissonance theory also applies to these types of rituals: *effort justification.* The more effort a person puts into a behavior that differs from their beliefs, the more power that behavior has to change those beliefs. You don't have to wear gloves filled with bullet ants to appreciate the power of effort justification. Almost anyone who's trained for a marathon, or given birth, or written a master's thesis has come away with both a heightened sense of their own capacities for self-control and perseverance and a belief that the end result justified the means to get there.

To make sure the prophecy continues to fulfill itself, though, it's important for the coming-of-age ritual to be followed by tangible changes in the adolescent's status, privileges, and duties. The community has to buy into the change, as when young Maasai men are given their own cattle. These ongoing markers of their new role remind both the new "adults" and the others around them that they're now mature members of the community. As we saw earlier, adulthood doesn't arrive in a particular moment in biological terms. It's a social construct, and everyone in the society has a hand in its construction and maintenance.

As we'll see, pain isn't the only way to show self-control. But many cultures and faiths use it because of its unique power to influence the minds and bodies of participants and onlookers alike. Perhaps the best evidence of this power comes from anthropologist Dimitris Xygalatas. Although the rituals he examines aren't rites of passage per se, they do share the element of extreme pain with the ones I've described.

To study how rituals using pain influence the mind, Xygalatas's team examined the Paso del Fuego, or fire-walking ritual, that is part of the Catholic celebration of San Juan in the Spanish town of San Pedro Manrique. As its name implies, the main event centers on people walking across several meters of smoldering coals with a temperature of around 1,250 degrees Fahrenheit. As Xygalatas's description of the event makes clear, firewalkers use strategies to cross the coals that are meant to minimize burns—strategies the novices learn from veterans. But even with the best strategies, it's not an easy feat. Those coals are still unbelievably *hot*.

As Xygalatas found, rituals involving pain have a deep physiological impact not just on the participants but upon the onlookers as well. To study this impact, his team placed unobtrusive, portable heart monitors on participants and observers at the fire-walking ritual.

In preparation for the main event, the fire walkers dance in a circle. Then, one by one, they hoist another person onto their backs for added weight before they traverse the glowing coals. Once they reach the other side, each person again steps on the cool earth to cheers from the onlookers. It's a time for anxiety but also celebration. When the last walk is done, the entire community joins in a raucous party.

As you might expect, everyone—walkers and observers alike—had quicker heart rates during the walks, some almost as high as two hundred beats per minute. Yet even in the face of this heightened arousal, most people reported that they felt calm—almost in a zen-like state—during these same periods. Yes, their hearts were racing, but their minds were not. Everyone was singularly focused on the efforts of the fire walkers.

An even more remarkable finding: as the heart rates of the fire walkers changed before, during, and after their walk across the coals, the audience's did the *same*. Everyone's physiology was synchronized. What's more, the degree of synchronization paralleled the social distances among people. As a fire walker's heart rate changed, so did the heart rates of all those watching. But the "tightness" of the linkage depended on how close people felt to the fire walker. For example, the heart rate of a fire walker's spouse would track changes more closely than that of a stranger's. In short, Xygalatas found a bodily linkage that creates new social bonds and strengthens existing ones.

Through the intense arousal they produce in both participants and observers, these rites accomplish two goals. By increasing mental focus on the events of the rite, they make the demonstration of self-control harder to forget. And by creating a type of physiological synchrony, they forge a sense of community between observers and fire walkers. As one fire walker told Xygalatas at the end of the ceremony, "Everyone is your brother."

Fortunately, pain isn't the only fuel on which rites of passage run.

By Brain

In the previous chapter, we saw that as societies became more complex, their understanding of God changed too. People envisioned a more omniscient, moralistic deity. One who began to place more emphasis on ethical attributes—a change that paralleled the needs of growing societies. In line with these changing needs, rites of passage evolved to focus on self-control in the intellectual and ethical realms—areas that tend to be more central to success in complex societies. These types of self-control can be readily shown through dedication to learning a faith's edicts and embodying its tenets. The process of becoming a *bar mitzvah*, or "son of the commandment," in Judaism is a case in point.

"Blessed be He who has released me from being liable for this boy." Since Talmudic times—a period spanning the first six centuries of the Common Era—this was the prayer a Jewish father would recite on his son's thirteenth birthday—the age when a boy would become a bar mitzvah and be judged according to his own actions. And in the early years of this period, that's about all a father would do to mark his son's coming of age.

Over time, as the importance of knowledge and religious obligation grew stricter, age-based rules for taking part in rituals became emphasized. During the Middle Ages, for example, children were no longer allowed to come to the bimah—the raised platform at the front of a synagogue—to read from the Torah or recite a blessing. And during the sixteenth century, in some places, wearing the tefillin (small boxes containing the words of the Shema prayer that are typically wrapped around the head and arm during morning worship) by minors also became frowned upon. With these changes, the importance of becoming a bar mitzvah increased, as it offered a clear signal that a young adult had achieved the knowledge necessary to take part fully in the religious life and responsibilities of the community. No longer was it simply the age at which a father was released from moral responsibility for his son.

With this change in emphasis, the ritual aspects of the ceremony became more elaborate and drew in the boys themselves. They were expected to develop the skills that would allow them to recite portions of the Torah when they were invited to the bimah for the first time. In many places, they were also encouraged to offer a *drasha*, or analytical discourse, about the readings. The community valued knowledge and virtue as markers of success in adulthood, so boys were called on to prove they had such qualities.

In today's world, there is no one specific format of rites a boy performs to become a bar mitzvah. In practice, though, most work something like the this. Boys spend years in religious instruction, learning how to read the Torah (especially if Hebrew is not their native language) and recite the blessings. On the big day, they go to the bimah for the first time and read from the Torah, sometimes also giving a discourse, and then celebrate with the community. In a welcome nod to gender equality, many forms of Judaism also celebrate girls becoming a bat mitzvah— "daughter of the commandment"—using a similar ceremony.

These rituals pull the same psychological levers as the other rites of passage we've seen. Here, demonstrating self-control centers not on withstanding pain or hardship but on acquiring knowledge through intellectual and moral fortitude. Kids study for years, attend prayer services, and the like rather than endure pain for days or months.

High arousal also plays a role in both sorts of ritual. While it's true that physical pain isn't involved in the Jewish rite, almost every bar or bat mitzvah feels their heart beating in their chest as they speak in front of a congregation for the first time. So, too, do their nervous parents and by extension, though to a lesser degree, other onlookers who don't want them to fail. Just as in Xygalatas's findings, here we'd also expect that the heartbeats of the audience should synchronize with those of the anxious teen, with the arousal focusing everyone's attention on them and the synchrony enhancing feelings of connection.

In some ways, though, the resulting change in social roles that follows this ritual isn't quite the same as those that follow many of the rituals that rely on pain. This isn't a criticism but an acknowledgment of how more modern societies function. On the day after someone becomes a bar or bat mitzvah, they're not treated much differently than they were on the day before. Sure, they can now perform certain religious duties meant for adults. But they still can't vote. They can't have their own bank accounts. Their friends and community treat them mostly the same way. And precisely because there is no readily observable change, the notion of being an adult either fades somewhat or exists only in narrow domains. The only way for a self-fulfilling prophecy to work—for a new identity to be reinforced and thus maintained—is for the message that things have changed to be repeated widely and often. When it's not, a rite of passage's effect on the psyche becomes muted.

This isn't an issue only for Judaism. It applies to Christian confirmation too. As with Judaism, there was no major historical emphasis on a rite of passage in early Christianity. Yet, through time, the sacrament of confirmation was modified to fill that psychological niche—the need to mark a person's readiness to take on the moral responsibilities of adulthood.

In the early Catholic Church, converts were confirmed in a ritual that gave them the gifts of the Holy Spirit: wisdom, knowledge, fortitude, piety, and fear of God. As a set, these gifts were meant to help them progress in their faith and in life. This rite immediately followed baptism, in which people descended into water as a way to cleanse their souls. Once a person was baptized, a religious leader would lay his hands upon them and anoint their head with holy oil before welcoming them into the community. But as Catholicism became a more established religion, many more people were born into it rather than entering through conversion. And so confirmation, along with baptism, tended to occur in infancy rather than in adulthood.

As the Middle Ages changed Jews' approach to becoming bar mitzvahs, that era altered Catholic ritual too. Confirmation was moved to adolescence, where it became a sign of spiritual maturity—a mark that a believer was ready to assume the moral responsibilities of adult life. Theologically, the focus was still on the gifts God provided. But psychologically, the notion of a general, not just spiritual, coming of age was difficult to ignore.

But today, if we're looking to these rites as true markers of leaving childhood behind, their power is limited, at least in comparison to some of the rituals we considered earlier. One reason why being confirmed or becoming a bar or bat mitzvah might not have the same effect is fairly straightforward: the corresponding rituals weren't originally meant to help teens become adults. In the more complex societies in which these rites arose, it often didn't make sense to have a single age at which full adulthood began.

Take the United States. In many states, you can start working at fourteen, can legally marry at sixteen or eighteen (though the cultural norm is much later), can vote or enter the armed forces at eighteen, can drink or smoke at twenty-one, and can remain a dependent on a parent's health insurance policy until twenty-six. Accordingly, the time it takes to complete an education and become financially independent can range from the late teens into the late twenties.

I'm not decrying the gradual onset of adulthood in many societies. To the contrary, I think it makes great sense. The social and economic opportunities and responsibilities that go with becoming an adult vary a good deal. If a single age for making the transition made more sense, I think the major religions of the world would have settled on more powerful rites to ease or solidify the change. But, in many ways, they're playing catch-up to societies that are rapidly altering their norms for adulthood—norms that are still in the process of evolving as economies change. Birth and death happen the same way now as in the past. Grief too. But defining maturity continues to be a work in progress, both for religions and for the societies they guide believers through.

Merit Badges

The most pertinent question to ask about rites of passage isn't whether they're effective. As we've seen, their effect varies based on several factors. Rather, the question to ask is how we might maximize their effectiveness. And in today's world, the answer concerns both timing—*when*—and frequency—*whens*.

An incremental approach to adulting fits better with what actually happens in people's lives and brains. Our frontal lobes—the parts that play a central role in abstract planning, reasoning, and impulse control—continue to develop through adolescence and into the early twenties. And with that growth comes cognitive capabilities that are essential to long-term planning and maturity—capabilities that can be reinforced in a cumulative way as a person faces the various challenges adulthood presents. In fact, the newest understanding of brain development suggests that it is more sensitive to rewards during adolescence than at any other time of life—a fact that makes the teenage mind especially malleable with respect to feedback from others. It is, in essence, a brain ready to be molded by rewards for taking on new roles.

But just because a onetime, one-size ritual might not be the best way to leave childhood behind doesn't mean that we have to ignore the insights that such rites provide. Teens in the modern world can certainly benefit from coming-of-age rituals; they just need to be more targeted and age appropriate—and repeated. Remember, the Sateré-Mawé require their boys to wear the bullet-ant gloves many times over several months. While this can be seen as one elongated ritual with initiates repeating the same act again and again, I'd argue that it's better understood as a series of separate rituals that repeatedly reinforce the transition to adulthood.

In thinking about how best to adapt or create rites of passage, let me say that I'm not in favor of using pain. While I recognize the psychological power that can come through experiences of pain and fatigue, I think there are better ways to achieve the same ends—ways that evoke effort and intense feelings but don't cause any physical or emotional harm.

If we want to help adolescents on the path to adulthood, I suggest that we consider using an incremental series of rituals explicitly tied to specific milestones. For example, in addition to rituals marking a time when a person becomes morally or religiously responsible, like those for becoming a bar or bat mitzvah or being confirmed, there could be additional ceremonies that mark a readiness for other responsibilities: a readiness to begin a first job, to date, to vote, to leave home for college, or to support oneself. Each should have a component that requires young people to show their growing capacity for self-control and perseverance (e.g., studying, saving a specific amount of money, completing a service project for the community, acquiring a specific ability through hard work), a ritualistic component that has young people stand before family and friends to show the fruits of their efforts and be acknowledged for them, and a postritual component where the family or even wider community acknowledges the change in status by modifying their expectations for the newly transformed.

That ritual itself should evoke emotion among the star and the audience alike. For example, parents can express their pride in their children, which will reinforce the pride their children feel in reaching the latest milestone. People can use music and singing to create synchrony, and thus a feeling of connection, among all involved. Perhaps the star could give a speech, as few activities better evoke strong arousal and emotions than taking the spotlight in front of peers and elders.

In many ways, what I'm describing here resembles Jewish and

Christian coming-of-age rites. But unlike what I'm recommending, those rites happen once and are often out of sync with the multiple incremental changes that are part of adolescence. Because these rituals focus primarily on religious responsibility and spiritual development, there is little change in what people expect of initiates in other domains of their lives at twelve or thirteen, when they're understandably viewed as not fully mature.

Some readers might dismiss my suggestions here for their seeming hokeyness. And I'd understand their reticence. But as we saw at the start of this book, even newly invented, completely arbitrary rituals can alter the mind. The trick is to figure out how to put the pieces together in the best way. Perhaps nobody has managed this trick better than Scouts BSA—the new name for the Boy Scouts of America in recognition of its recent welcoming of young women to the fold.

The highest, and in many ways most transformative, change in rank a teen can receive is recognition as an Eagle Scout. It's an honor awarded after the scout has shown commitments to duty toward God and country, to help others, to keep physically and mentally fit, and to remain morally upstanding—all qualities that require self-control and ones that most of us would consider hallmarks of responsible adulthood.

Achieving this status is no easy feat. The twenty-one challenges a scout must master include success in personal fitness and management, family life, first aid, citizenship, environmental sustainability, emergency preparedness, cooking, camping, communication skills, and local and global citizenship. In addition, a scout must also complete a long-term service project that will benefit a religious institution, school, or community.

Few can doubt that clearing these high bars requires a good deal of self-control and effort. As such, they're ripe to nudge a scout's mind toward adulting. Becoming an Eagle Scout is also an honor that is recognized and valued by communities at large. Many employers look upon Eagle Scout status quite favorably, and many Eagle Scouts go on to find success in life.

My main point here isn't to extol Scouting BSA per se. As an institution, it's had its problems. Rather, my point is to show how the frameworks certain religions use to usher teens into adulthood can be adapted to the circumstances of modern life. Much as scouting offers merit badges and ceremonies for those who successfully meet specific challenges, so, too, might we construct rituals to acknowledge whatever milestones we deem to be important during the journey of adolescence. By making the ritual a series of steps instead of a full jump, it becomes easier for teens (and their parents) to build confidence along the way. The pride that comes with mastering each step will make taking the next step more appealing. We already do some of this now with sports, where teens progress through several stages (e.g., freshman, junior varsity, then varsity), but fully ritualizing the process, and making it applicable to many domains of life, will help build more fully rounded adults.

It's not up to me to decide what age or ages are best suited for these steps. Even within a given culture, tying them to a specific age may not make sense. Different teens often develop according to their own clocks, meaning that the date for any rite might best be left to a family's choosing. But a teen crossing each threshold and marking that both by ceremony and symbol can only help ease their path toward maturity. In this way, others will know where any teen stands on that twisty path and what's fair to expect of them. And while adopting such practices on a larger scale might take a movement—in many ways, that's what a religion *is*—you can start in your family or group of friends right now. After all, that's how movements begin.

4

Transcending the Twenties and Thirties: Love, Connection, and (Maybe) Ecstasy

Adulthood brings with it freedom and responsibility—and a need to establish new connections. While the new adult has usually not abandoned family ties altogether, those ties are almost always more tenuous than they were during childhood. To retain or regain a sense of intimate connection, most people look for romance. Some, though, look for something even deeper: a mystical connection with the divine.

It might seem strange that I'm talking about marriage and mysticism in the same place. Many people probably wouldn't put them together. And I'd understand why. While marriages, and the rituals that surround them, serve two purposes—a practical one and a spiritual one—we tend to focus more on the former. Most people see weddings as marking a change in social roles. Across the globe, the basic framework for wedding rituals is much the same. As friends and family look on, couples recite vows to love and support one another before a religious officiant, receive a blessing, and then put on a symbol of their new status—almost always a ring. Whether the ritual takes place under a chuppah as in Judaism, before an altar as in Christianity, or around a ceremonial fire as in Hinduism, it's all about marking a change in social roles.

The fact that weddings change people's roles might make them seem similar to the rituals we discussed in the last chapter. And, in fact, they are. A wedding *is* a rite of passage. It assigns new roles and responsibilities to people. But unlike the rites of passage I described before that mark peoples' moves toward independence, the spiritual aspect of weddings moves people toward interdependence. In its truest form, marriage is designed to foster what may be the deepest feeling of connection there is—a connection that's experienced as almost a complete merging of identities. And that's where the link with mysticism—the experience of transcendent connection—comes in.

But marriages aren't the same as weddings. Where weddings are a rite of passage—a kind of one-and-done event (at least with each partner)—marriages are enduring relationships. The real work of creating and maintaining connection isn't done by wedding ceremonies but by practices that come after it—practices that allow people to grow together over time. It's these practices and rituals that I'll focus on here. Because whether we're talking about connection with a spouse or a deity, the joy, love, and, if you're lucky, transcendence that come with it can satisfy some of the deepest yearnings humans experience. Yearnings for union and meaning.

There are many routes to achieve intense connection, but all of them require a simultaneous manipulation of the body and mind. Sometimes it's through intense meditation, sometimes through psychedelics, sometimes through dance, and sometimes through sex. Although in this context, the focus of sexual intimacy isn't on pleasure or procreation.

Most religions, even the stodgier ones, recognize the power that sexual intimacy can have. As couples exchange wedding rings in the Church of England, they say "With my body I honor you, all that I am I give to you, and all that I have I share with you, within the love of God." Note that that bodily honoring comes first here. The biblical Song of Songs (which Christianity and Judaism both treat as holy scripture) extols the intense joy that physical intimacy offers: "Let him kiss me with the kisses of his mouth: for thy love is better than wine. . . . Draw me, we will run after thee: the king hath brought me into his chambers: we will be glad and rejoice in thee, we will remember thy love more than wine . . ." Clearly, sex can be sacred.

For these reasons, almost all religions recognize that the physical can be a vehicle for the spiritual. Through the ages, mystics have used techniques that rely on the body to achieve communion with the divine. And when they do, their experience of God's love or a feeling of merging with the oneness that joins all creation can be just as pleasurable and profound as the connection between lovers.

This type of deep connection doesn't come easily. It's not automatic. If it were, casual sex and dropping acid would fundamentally change people's lives for the better. Safe to say: they don't. The conditions have to be just right. Preparation and having a guide are key to success. During the time of life when many are seeking a new type of connection, finding the right guidance and techniques are paramount. Fortunately, many religions offer both.

Tantra Isn't for Turtles

For many people, the word "tantra" brings to mind techniques for enhancing sexual pleasure. And if you google "tantra," you'll find lots of links to *Cosmopolitan*, Goop, and other wellness sites that present it mostly in this context. They might give a quick nod to its spiritual potential, but most of the discussion will focus on physical ecstasy.

In its original incarnation, though, tantra wasn't about pleasure. It was a set of beliefs and techniques meant to break people out of their normal patterns of thought and ways of seeing the world. The goal was to foster a direct experience with the divine. While some tantric techniques involved taboo practices (e.g., eating meat or drinking alcohol if your religion usually forbade it, sitting on a corpse to meditate on death), others relied on direct manipulations of the body to achieve altered states. All of them were meant to help people feel a sense of communion with something greater than themselves.

When it comes to tantric techniques, the ones that leverage the body's wiring—and an easy way to do that is via sex—use a deep feeling of connection with another person as a jumping-off point to that greater transcendent experience. And either or both these types of connection can banish the loneliness that life sometimes brings, especially as people strike out on their own.

Because they use the body to manipulate the mind, most tantric sexual techniques focus on physical elements. They share an emphasis on deep breathing and breath control, touch and massage, affirming mutual eye gazes, and synchronous movement. The goal isn't to rush to climax; it's to bond and connect as those taking part lose themselves in each other.

Like many spiritual technologies, the tools that make up tantric sex are well-thought-out: the combined implementation of the breathing, the massaging, the gazing, and the bodily syncing exerts a specific influence on the mind. You can think of it as a "connection hack," because that's exactly how it operates. To see why, we first need to take a brief look at how the human body is wired for connection.

Polyvagal theory (PVT) provides a perfect lens for viewing the physiology of connection. In Latin, *vagus* means wandering, and that's an apt name for the body's longest nerve. After leaving the brain stem, the vagus nerve snakes through the body, extending its fibers to a host of muscles and organs: parts of the mouth and throat, the heart, the lungs, the stomach, and the intestines, to name a few. The vagus nerve also does double duty: it delivers information from the body to the brain as it conveys orders from the brain to the body.

The vagus nerve has two branches. The more ancient one is common to most animals. Reptiles have it; so do fish. Its purpose is simple: to keep the animal from harm by activating the fight-or-flight system. It elevates heart rate and breathing so that animals can escape threats. Or, when escape is all but impossible, it makes animals play dead or faint, as most predators avoid eating carrion.

Animals aren't always being preyed upon, of course. They have less stressful periods too. If you're a turtle, lizard, or frog, there's not that much else you need to do during much of this time except feed. Otherwise, except for a quick, nonintimate mating here and there, best to sit tight, conserve your energy, or keep looking for some food. But if you're a mammal, and especially if you're a human, sitting alone isn't helpful. Many would consider it problematic. It's through building and reinforcing social connections that most mammals improve their situation in life. It's how we humans form the bonds necessary for our survival and well-being.

And that's why we, unlike turtles and the like, have a second, newer branch of the vagus nerve to help us thrive.

This newer branch has three primary functions. The first centers on the heart and its ties to respiration. As activity in the vagus—also known as vagal tone—increases, a person's heart rate and respiration slow. The second function centers on the endocrine system. As vagal tone goes up, the release of stress hormones in the body goes down. Higher vagal tone works like a brake on our physiology; it calms us. The third function centers on communication. Increased vagal tone enhances emotional expression in the face, the inner ear's ability to tune itself to the frequencies most associated with human speech, and the larynx's ability to relax and produce tones in a more soothing range. All told, heightened vagal tone primes people to socialize, communicate, and connect.

There's a good deal of research showing that increased vagal tone supports stronger and more empathic bonds between people. In children, for example, heightened vagal tone predicts more positive emotions, fewer problematic behaviors toward others, and increased social skills. In adults, greater vagal tone is associated with better social connectedness, enhanced well-being, and greater empathy for others. And in the case of romantic love, a couple's vagal tone becomes regularly elevated—a calming of cardiac reactivity that works to buttress them against stress.

Religions have found ways to manipulate vagal tone in order to increase our sense of connection and empathy, perhaps most notably in the practice of tantric sex. When couples follow tantric practice, intentionally slowing and deepening their breathing, caressing each other and gazing into each other's eyes, their heart rates decrease as their vagal tones rise. Tantric sex is less about orgasm than it is about creating a transcendent sense of connection.

Direct manipulation of vagal tone through touch, breath control, and gaze aren't the only arrows tantric sex has in its quiver. It also changes people's physiological states via synchronization. Psychophysiologists have known for decades that as the physical distance between people decreases, their bodily rhythms begin to mirror one another. Their breathing and heart rates become synchronized. As we've seen, greater synchronization creates a stronger sense of connection. As two lovers begin to align their movements, it becomes easier for each person to predict the other's thoughts and feelings. Synchrony helps intuition as bodily states begin to match.

Connection works the other way too. Synchrony doesn't just make people feel closer to each other; how close they emotionally feel at the start of any encounter can also affect synchrony. For example, studies show that conversing couples' heart rhythms, respiration rates, and vagal tones tend to synchronize, but the fidelity of the linkage—the degree to which the physiological signals move in lockstep between the partners—depends on their marital satisfaction. The happier they are with each other, the more their bodily states mirror each other. Over time, this means that as each act of tantric sex brings lovers closer, it also sets up the next encounter to provide an even stronger experience of connection.

Unlike some spiritual practices, the elements of tantric sex don't need to be closely tied to specific theological principles. They rely more on controlling the body to influence the mind. Like meditation, tantric practice is adaptable to a variety of purposes and faiths. There's a new breed of Christian sex coaches who teach these techniques and professors at major Christian universities who are researching their history and the role sex might have played in early Judeo-Christian thought. Removing Hindu and Buddhist religious notions doesn't alter the way tantric techniques affect the body and mind. As we'll see with meditation, the practice can work without the theology. So if you're interested in this route to connection with a partner, these tools are quite easy to incorporate.

But what about transcendence? If you're using tantric sex to connect with more than just your partner, an altered state of consciousness has to be involved somewhere. Here's where the rhythmic aspect of tantric sex comes in. The synchronized groove that tantric lovers attain doesn't only produce a deep sense of bonding; it also can change conscious experience. Sustained rhythmic, physical stimulation leads to neural entrainment—an alignment of neural signals that produces an explosion in brain activity. If you think of the brain as a blob with electrical pulses running through it, neural entrainment means that the pulses don't seem random. They seem to be occurring in time with each other, as if the whole brain is pulsing to the same rhythm. As these pulses mirror each other, they reinforce each other until the power of this signal interferes with the normal operation of the brain.

This change in the brain's normal electrical patterns can alter how people experience the world. Your brain interprets the information that comes in from your eyes, ears, and other sense organs. So when your brain gets hijacked, so, too, do your senses. The result is that lovers will feel not only closer to each other but further from everyday reality. They might suddenly sense the divine with the same kind of clarity and immediacy with which they usually feel the normal world every day. This is the original purpose of tantra and why—despite its R-rated reputation in some quarters—it qualifies fully as a spiritual practice. It's to this transcendent mystical experience of connection that we now turn.

Mystics, Monastics, and Mushrooms

When most people think of mystics or monastics, "connection" isn't the first word that usually comes to mind. By definition, these people are less focused on the normal rhythms of social life to which most of us adhere. But they're seeking connection nonetheless: connection with the divine. People who go down this path don't want to study or simply pray to God; they want to directly experience It. They want to break the chains of mundane, normal reality and sense the universe in its vast, grand totality. They want to embrace that which created it, that which defines it, that which, in daily life, seems beyond grasp.

This desire isn't specific to any one religion. Almost all faiths offer techniques to those who want to forge such an intimate bond with the divine. At a broad level, you can divide these techniques into what have been termed right-handed and left-handed approaches. The right-handed approaches fit more easily within the traditional branches of their respective religions. They focus on practices meant to alter consciousness, such as meditation and asceticism. Left-handed approaches have a little more shock value. They're designed to break down illusions of duality by pushing the envelope of experience and rule breaking. Participants might drink or smoke substances that lead to hallucinations, place ashes of the dead on their bodies, or eat foods that are taboo in their faiths. Here again, hedonism or chaos aren't the goals of the rituals. Rather, it's to provide participants with experiences whose intensity and transgressive nature might shatter conventional assumptions about how the world works. In those moments of shattered assumptions, the mind can embrace new ways of thinking and seeing the world.

Although each religion bases its practices on a different set of beliefs, the resulting mystical experiences are usually quite similar.

Mystical states are described either as a feeling of union with the divine or as a dissolution of the self into nothingness. And while these two descriptions might appear at odds with one another, that too is a bit of an illusion—one that's predicated on time.

In comparing Eastern and Western approaches to mysticism, it's tempting to assume that the experience of the former differs from the latter. Whereas Judeo-Christian theology speaks of an active, intentional God with whom to personally connect, Buddhism emphasizes emptiness and the peace that comes from merging with it. But if you look closely at the descriptions of mystical experiences from Christian sources, they increasingly resemble those from Buddhist sources as the practitioner progresses. The sense of self dissolves in both cases.

Many of the most famous Christian mystics—from Pseudo-Dionysius the Areopagite, to Meister Eckhart, to Saint Teresa of Ávila—talk about transcendence arriving in a series of steps. The earlier ones involve a feeling of love or even spiritual ecstasy that comes from a direct connection with God. Saint Teresa's description of one of her most celebrated visions captures it well:

> I saw in his [an angel's] hand a long spear of gold, and at the iron's point there seemed to be a little fire. He appeared to me to be thrusting it at times into my heart, and to pierce my very entrails; when he drew it out, he seemed to draw them out also, and to leave me all on fire with a great love of God. The pain was so great, that it made me moan; and yet so surpassing was the sweetness of this excessive pain, that I could not wish to be rid of it. The soul is satisfied now with nothing less than God. The pain is not bodily, but spiritual; though the body has its share in it, even a large one. It is a caressing of love so sweet which now takes place between

the soul and God, that I pray God of His goodness to make him experience it who may think that I am lying.

This feeling of passionate connection to God is as common among Sufi Muslims or Silicon Valley ayahuasca consumers as it is among Christian mystics. But as people continue down any faith's mystical path, the later stages are defined by a dissolution into nothingness—an absorption into God as Saint Teresa described her later experiences, or a merging with the "Godhead" as Meister Eckhart referred to it. In this advanced stage of transcendence, consciousness disappears in a way that looks remarkably similar among different faiths. The Christian notion of merging with the Godhead jibes closely with the Hindu idea of melding with Brahma—the force underlying all of reality—and the Buddhist of attaining nirvana.

In progressing from an initial state that Saint Teresa describes as akin to communing with a lover to one described as merging with an unknowable divine, we're seeing a reflection of how tantric sex also moves the mind. While the methods are entirely different, the psychological experiences echo one another.

It's no accident that some mystic practices evoke a feeling of loving connection with a divine force before people lose their sense of self. While one isn't necessary for the other, the ordered pairing—the feeling of comfort before nothingness—is an example of a spiritual technology at its best. Feeling your sense of self dissolve, a phenomenon sometimes referred to as ego death, can be quite disorienting. Frightening, in fact. Sensing reality changing in front of your eyes—not knowing where you begin or end—can be the stuff of nightmares.

Such negative experiences can and do happen in the pursuit of transcendence—anxiety, paranoia, even outright terror. And while they're more common among people who use left-handed mystical techniques that rely on hallucinogens or other drugs, they can also beset people using right-hand ones. Twenty-five percent of meditators have suffered at least one bout of fear, anxiety, or depression as they confronted questions of emptiness and nonself. Of those, a small minority even feel their personhood shatter in a way that makes them wonder if they can put it back together. While some of these instances can be explained by preexisting mental illness, others result from poor instruction and preparation in using the techniques.

The best protection against the dangers of the mystical path is a sense of security. As the psychologists John Bowlby and Mary Ainsworth revealed decades ago, attachment is the key to feeling secure when exploring novel situations. Feeling someone or something is there to keep you safe while your views of reality shift allows your mind to be less fearful in the moment. It lets you open up to new and disorienting states precisely because you feel secure. This is why, as we'll see, the left-hand mystic rituals usually require the presence of a spiritual guide. This priest or shaman provides a scaffold for the mind—a guardrail of sorts to let people feel safe and to keep things on track as they imbibe hallucinogens or use other techniques to alter their consciousness. Without that guide, negative experiences are much more frequent.

Right-hand techniques like prayer and meditation also benefit from scaffolding. You still need an abbot, priest, or elder to teach the appropriate skills and to check in with you as your practice progresses. But after you achieve some competence, the rituals provide the protection you need mostly by themselves. The guide need no longer always be present. Like tantric sex, though using very different techniques, the rituals alter your physiology to make you feel connected and safe—a state from which you can move toward an experience of dissolution without anxiety or fear.

Many of those who pursue a mystical path via right-handed techniques do so through religious orders. They give over part or all of their lives to this pursuit, sequestering themselves in cloisters that offer unparalleled opportunities to focus on their goals. For most people, monastic life centers around a daily schedule of prayer, contemplation, and ceremonial activity. But within each, the prescribed rituals and practices target the same physiological response: increased vagal activity. And when people perform these rituals together, they also enhance synchrony, which boosts the sense of security that can be crucial in achieving that elusive, ecstatic sense of oneness with the divine.

Consider meditation. While we think of it as primarily a Buddhist practice, many religions use it. Some forms, especially the Christian ones, start by focusing on a scriptural passage. Others contemplate specific teachings, puzzle-like koans, or the physical sensations of one's own body. But irrespective of the exact form, almost all types of meditation incorporate a period of stillness where one withdraws from the constant parade of disparate thoughts and emotions that constitute ordinary consciousness.

Lectio divina is one of the better-known forms of Christian meditation. It consists of four steps. In the first, *lectio*, a person reads a short passage from scripture aloud, paying attention to each word. In the second step, *meditatio*, the passage is read again, but now with a very intentional and unhurried consideration of its deeper meaning—the broader message that God is offering the reader. In the third, *oratio*, the person now responds to God's message with prayer, sometimes reading the passage yet again while thanking God for the message and guidance. In the final phase, *contemplatio*, the conscious interaction with God ceases. It's a period for silently resting in the presence of the unknowable divine. *Contemplatio* is often described as a time for letting all thought go and communing with God in a way that feels as if there's a merging of oneself into His power and love.

Whichever form of meditation you choose, you'll find that, just like tantric techniques, it uses the body's neural wiring to achieve its goal. One way it does this is by altering breathing. Buddhist techniques offer specific instruction on how to breathe while sitting silently. As people take deeper and deeper breaths, their respiration rate will slow and their diaphragms will be pushed downward into their bellies. Both of these actions increase vagal tone, which starts a cascade of physiological changes that relax the body and move the mind toward a state of openness. For this reason, it's not surprising that researchers have documented both immediate and, for regular practitioners, longer-term elevations in vagal tone as a consequence of meditation.

There are other ways to control the breath. In *lectio divina*, breaths become slower, deeper, and more regular through recitations of prayer and readings from scripture. While it might not be immediately apparent that reading aloud slows respiration, it is a proven fact. When researchers compared the cardiac and respiratory activity of people as they said the Hail Mary prayer using the rosary, recited Hindu mantras, talked casually to someone, or simply sat in a chair, they found that while respiration rates were a bit slower during casual conversation than when people let their minds wander while sitting quietly, reciting structured prayers and mantras reduced the rate even more.

Whereas people took about fourteen breaths per minute spontaneously, that rate dropped to six per minute when praying. Each breath was also deeper, meaning it depressed the diaphragm to a greater extent. The resulting change in the body and mind was the same: heart rates and breathing slowed as the brain calmed and became more open to connection. Here again, we see a spiritual technology working at its peak. One of the ingenious elements of the *lectio divina* is that its earlier phases—the ones involving slow, intentional recitations and prayer—make the body and brain more receptive to the last phase: the experience of a positive connection with the divine during the silent *contemplatio*.

In monasteries and temples, people don't only meditate or pray in isolation. Buddhist monks often meditate together in large halls. Every day, Christian monks sing hymns and chant prayers as parts of communal ceremonies. In these cases, the effects on breathing don't only increase vagal tone because of people's individual actions, but also because of the social nature of the rituals. We know, for instance, that the vagal tone and breathing patterns of choir members become more synchronized as they sing. And the resulting synchrony between people, much as with tantric sex, in turn continues to elevate vagal tone for all involved. The result is a sense of bliss and connection to one another as voices repetitively intermingle and merge.

The very design of holy places like monasteries magnifies the effects of the rituals that occur within them. They lack the intrusions, the noise, and the distractions that are so common to daily life. CNN isn't blaring with breaking news. *The New York Times* isn't arriving daily with accounts of new horrors. It's quite the opposite. These sacred spaces exude timelessness and peace. And the people who inhabit these places try to echo that peacefulness. They dress simply and treat one another respectfully. All in all, it's an environment that feels calming, inspiring, and safe.

As I noted at the beginning of this book, the brain is a prediction machine. Even when you're not consciously aware of it, your mind is sussing out your environs and preparing you for what might happen next. This under-the-radar surveillance and inference also influence vagal activity. Remember, information travels two ways along the vagus: top-down and bottom-up.

This bidirectional pathway means that your mind isn't just influenced by manipulations of the body, but can alter vagal tone through its predictions of the future—a fact that monastic design exploits, as does the architecture of many places of worship. As you enter these places, your mind takes in the signals of safety emitted by the tranquil environs. Because it now feels safe and assumes that no threats are likely to emerge here, your mind then sends commands to the body that increase vagal tone even more. This back-and-forth along the vagus promotes a calm acceptance and an openness to connection and new experiences. That's the perfect state in which to seek transcendence.

These right-handed mystical methods—the ones relying on prayer, meditation, and often monastic seclusion—consist of two steps on the path to transcendence, with the first setting up a protective scaffold for the second. Those who follow it first come to feel love and a sense of security before serenely taking the next step into the great unknown of nothingness. Physiologically, though, it's a story of the body calmly and confidently preparing for a different state of consciousness. And it's here, if we look at a neurological level, that we can see what rigorous meditation training can do to the mind to help foster that mystical sense of connecting with God or of self-dissolution.

Over the past decade, it's become clear that meditation alters activity in the brain's default mode network (DMN). As the name suggests, this network can be identified by a specific pattern of interconnected activity across several brain regions—one that's typically found when the mind is resting. "Resting" in this context means the mind is wandering. It's daydreaming. It's thinking about the past or planning for the future. Basically all the stuff that meditation tries to evade so that people can be perfectly present.

If meditation is doing its job, we'd expect people to show less activity in the DMN while they meditate. That's exactly what neuroscientists have found. During meditation, expert meditators' DMN activity is substantially lower than that of novices. Not only does this pattern signify a state of greater presence and less distraction, but also, given the established link between activity in the DMN and thoughts about oneself, a state of decreased focus on personal identity. In other words, the reduced DMN activity of meditators creates perfect conditions for losing awareness of one's self.

Moving toward that transcendence doesn't require sitting on a cushion or bench, even when using a right-handed approach. While most Christians and Buddhists pursue it that way, other traditions have found different ways to disrupt the DMN. The Islamic mystics known as Sufis don't sit; they whirl. After first chanting and reciting prayers together, many Sufis begin to spin— turning again and again like a top. While the rhythmic chanting that accompanies the ritual synchronizes physiology and increases vagal tone, the spinning—something that would make most people quickly feel dizzy—brings on an altered state. Over time, the brains of Sufis actually change in form. They show a reduced cortical thickness in areas central to the DMN, as well as shrinkage in other brain areas that track movement—a change that allows the Sufi to spin himself into an altered state of consciousness without getting dizzy or sick.

Hindu mystics also practice very active forms of mysticism. For millennia, many Hindus pursing transcendence have relied on yoga to support their journey. I don't mean the various types of yoga now popular in the West, but a more complex and demanding type that is paired with a focus on mantra recitation and contemplation. By placing the body in specific poses while controlling breathing, yoga increases vagal tone. And that physiological change, when combined with fixing the mind's attention on mantras, works similarly to most forms of meditation: it can provide a scaffold of security as the sense of self melts away.

These two elements—the scaffolding and the melting—unite successful approaches to mysticism across religions. But while right-handed mystical paths can be quite effective, they do take time to learn. Left-handed approaches can be far quicker. They can work in hours, as opposed to months or years.

Of the many left-handed approaches to transcendence, psychoactive substances are among the most popular. For centuries, Indigenous peoples of South America have used a botanical brew called ayahuasca as a spiritual medicine—one that can heal psychological wounds or offer insight by fundamentally reshaping perceptions of the world and deconstructing the sense of self. Yet for all its power, ayahuasca isn't pleasant. It's a bitter and yeasty brew made by boiling the vines of *Banisteriopsis caapi* and the leaves of *Psycotria viridis*. The combo is necessary, because although the leaves of *P. Viridis* contain the hallucinogen N,N-Dimethyltryptamine, better known as DMT, this chemical is quickly deactivated by a digestive enzyme in the stomach. The vines of *B. Caapi* contain a chemical that inhibits this digestive enzyme from degrading DMT, thereby allowing the hallucinogen to enter the bloodstream and reach the brain.

One of the things I find most interesting about ayahuasca is that its DMT affects the brain in a similar way to meditation: it reduces activity in the default mode network. Within forty minutes of ingesting ayahuasca, the DMN begins to quiet. So in addition to causing visual and auditory hallucinations, the DMT in ayahuasca directly targets the parts of the brain from which our sense of self springs. In so doing, it allows memories from within the mind to mix with perceptions coming in from the outside world, all the while blurring the whole into a seemingly fantastic concoction into which a coherent sense of self dissolves.

As you might well imagine, this potent mix can produce an unpredictable mental state. When it's good, ayahuasca can bring on feelings of deep and universal connection. But when it's bad, it can produce a disorienting horror show. Sean Illing, who writes for *Vox*, offered one of my favorite descriptions of these dual possibilities. He had decided to personally investigate the effects of ayahuasca before writing about it, and headed to a Costa Rican wellness center that offers ayahuasca retreats. During a ceremony one evening, he described how drinking the brew led him to vividly reexperience a beautiful event: the first time he and his wife made love. He could see the lake in front of them and smell the fresh air of the college campus where they were at the time. In that moment, he said, "There was no ego. I wasn't an isolated 'I,' a separate person with a separate consciousness." But then the vision turned darker. He could also see every moment in the relationship where his wife had reached out to him but he'd turned away. During ceremonies on other evenings, he felt blissful seeing himself floating in his mother's womb, but then, in the midst of the intense nausea ayahuasca typically evokes, his vision changed to one of seeing forty or more yellow snakes rush out of the mouth of a nearby person and into his own.

Such are the blessings and trials of ayahuasca. It can, like many right-handed techniques, make you feel a warm glow of connection before blowing your mind wide open in ways that let you see the world in a different light. But other times it can put you in what feels like a kaleidoscopic hellscape. The experience is almost always intense, but whether that intensity is enlightening or frightening depends on your preparation.

In reducing the time and effort necessary to reach transcendence, left-handed techniques are also more likely to pose a danger. By losing or breeching some of the guardrails that keep the mind safe—the careful modulations of vagal tone, the expert guidance of a teacher—there's more potential for things to go awry. With aya-huasca becoming more popular—pop-up rituals can be found almost daily in the tony neighborhoods of Silicon Valley and Brooklyn—this is a burgeoning problem. The use of powerful substances like these requires expert knowledge—one honed through centuries of use. And when the rituals are altered—when the wisdom of the original practitioners is disregarded—the risks become greater.

Traditionally, ayahuasca ceremonies were conducted by sha-mans, each of whom had undergone years of training. It was the shaman's job to guide people, to keep them safe during the violent purging that often takes place as a side effect, and to help them make sense of what they experience while in the potion's grasp. The shamans also usually sing *icaros*—complex, rhythmic, "magic" songs for healing—during the ceremonies and encourage people to join in. Here again, singing and chanting evokes comfort and syn-chronous states that scaffold the coming hallucinations and sense of ego death. And since ayahuasca has been shown to place people in a heightened state of mindfulness for up to twenty-four hours after ingestion, the guidance and interpretations the shamans offer have time to bake into people's minds as they reexperience their selfhood and reflect on whether and how their understanding of themselves and the world should change.

Magic mushrooms work in a similar way, though usually with much less vomiting. The "magic" in these mushrooms is the hal-lucinogen psilocybin. Like ayahuasca, psilocybin reduces activity the brain's DMN. And while several different types of mushrooms contain psilocybin—a fact made use of to varying degrees by dif-ferent cultures on different continents—some of the most well-known mushroom use centers on the species *Psilocybe aztecorum,* which the Aztecs called the god mushroom. Today the Mazatec people of Mexico have the longest tradition of using it.

For centuries, the Mazatec have practiced a faith that is a combination of the Roman Catholicism brought by the Spanish and the preexisting beliefs native to the area. At base, the way the Mazatecs use the mushrooms doesn't differ much from the ayahuasca script. It usually begins after sunset, with shamans leading rhythmic chants as people sit in circles clapping in time. After an hour or so of this synchronous music making, the shamans hand out the mushroom, which people eat. Not long after, the altered states begin, with the shamans keeping a close eye and helping people make sense of what is happening.

Within the mind, psilocybin works its magic just as ayahuasca does. At low levels, it produces visual, auditory, and tactile hallucinations. But at higher levels, it can lead to ego death. As it targets the DMN, people's sense of self dissolves, and with it, they experience a sense of merging with the natural world or the divine. Many users report their experiences with psilocybin as among the most significant of their entire lives.

While this may sound like hyperbole, it's not. In 2006, a team of psychopharmacologists at Johns Hopkins University examined the links between psilocybin and mystical experiences by having people actually ingest it in a lab. To make sure no one was intentionally trying to bring on or fake an altered state, the researchers used a double-blind design. During each session, neither the researchers nor the participants knew if the pills to be swallowed contained psilocybin or another drug (a mild stimulant). But before anyone took a pill, the researchers spent a good deal of time speaking with each participant to build a sense of confidence and trust. They also stayed with them during the session, acting as a modern-day shaman might by offering guidance and a sense of security during the disorienting experience that was unfolding.

A few hours after people took one of the pills, the researchers asked them about their experiences. For those who took psilocybin, the past few hours were a trip. They hallucinated with their eyes and their ears. But these trips weren't simply novel experiences; people reported they were imbued with a sense of sacredness. They were profoundly positive states that made people feel as if they had transcended time and space. But perhaps most significant of all was that when the research team reassessed people two months later, 71 percent of those who took psilocybin reported that the experience was one of the top five spiritual events they'd ever had. Sixty-seven percent reported that it was one of the top five most meaningful experiences in their entire lives. And, remember, this was just from popping a pill while sitting in a fairly sterile research lab. Imagine the added significance that could come from taking psilocybin within the context of a religious ritual.

By breaking down the sense of self, chemically induced mystical experiences, like the more rigorous meditation-derived ones coming from right-handed techniques, offer an opportunity to reformulate it—to fundamentally alter the way people see the world and their place in it. In fact, psilocybin use has been shown to make people more imaginative and welcoming of new ideas for up to a year after taking it. Like ayahuasca, though, positive experiences aren't guaranteed; they often require expert guidance.

Take My Hand

The urge for connection runs deep—so deep that it's embedded in the wiring of our brain and body. For Erik Erikson, one of the most famous developmental psychologists of the twentieth century, finding that connection is the preeminent challenge we face during our twenties and thirties. Meeting that challenge requires more than finding a partner; it means finding a soul mate. Someone, or in the case of those pursuing the mystical path, *something* with which you merge so fully that you can lose awareness of your own self. As the Sufi master Rumi argued, it's the concepts of "you" and "me" that prevent people from feeling the bliss of union: "I, you, he, she, we. In the garden of mystic lovers, these are not true distinctions."

If you're looking for a spiritual connection—whether on its own or as a complement to a bond with a partner—there are two ways to get there. You can take the right hand or the left. One isn't necessarily better than the other. They just work in different ways. Or you can take both hands. Many people pursue a rigorous meditative practice or carefully use psychedelics while also living in the "real world" far away from any cloister. Many non-Hindus are discovering how tantric sex can be a link to spirituality. By whatever route and along whatever timeline you follow, the ultimate reward, even if you can only experience it for a few moments, is transcendence.

That term might sound squishy or gauzy to some. But it is real. Even Albert Einstein, who didn't believe in a personal god, believed that a feeling of mystical transcendence was among the most beautiful and profound emotional experiences available to humankind. "He to whom this emotion is a stranger . . . is as good as dead," he wrote. Millions of people share his view to some degree, as the growing interest in meditation, ayahuasca, and psilocybin during the past decade proves.

For those who do choose to pursue the mystical experience, let me reassert my note of caution: it doesn't always go well without careful guidance. These practices need to be scaffolded. As Michael Pollan, who delved deeply into the history and use of psychedelics, has said, "When psychedelics like psilocybin and LSD burst upon the scene in the 1950s and 1960s, they arrived without an instruction manual. Half a century later, we're still struggling to learn how best to harness their spooky power." Pollan, like me, believes a way to reduce potential harms is to look to the cultures that have long used psychedelics for spiritual purposes. Through vast experience, they've developed a set of instructions—one that a Brooklyn hipster or Silicon Valley shaman might not know. And since Pollan notes that about 8 percent of people who have a "bad trip" end up seeking psychiatric care, finding the right guide for any attempt at transcendence is essential.

The same logic applies to meditation. McMindfulness, as today's cottage industry of meditation is often derisively termed, isn't likely to do people much good. In the corporate retreat versions, many traditional aspects have been removed. Yet, in its traditional form, not only does meditation increase a sense of connection to others, it can, over time, also bring on that unique feeling of transcendence.

Still, just because religions have developed ritual scaffoldings for these techniques doesn't mean the techniques can't be modified. It doesn't mean that the exact same *icaro* needs to be sung at every ayahuasca ceremony, or that the steps of *lectio divina* must be rigidly followed with respect to scriptural readings. Some of the content can be changed as long as the structure and goals remain the same. In fact, we see this with meditation itself. Both within Buddhism and even across religions, the exact forms of meditation—the mantras, the prayers, the symbols used—vary a great deal. But the underlying structure of the techniques—the quiet, the focus, the attention to breathing, the use of chanting or recitations—occurs frequently. The goal is to calm the body and focus the mind using techniques that modify human physiology.

It's the same with psychedelics. Roland Griffiths, one of the leading pharmacologists studying the links between psilocybin and mystical experiences, has shown, as we saw above, that even when people consume this hallucinogen in a lab, the result can still feel profoundly meaningful. In his most recent work, Griffiths found psilocybin can help heal the anxiety and depression that come from existential dread. In giving a single dose to people with advanced cancer, he determined that 75 percent of them reported a significant lifting of their spirits even when facing imminent death. They felt more connection, more compassion, and more gratitude for the people and the world around them. Many even began comforting worried relatives.

Griffiths also found that the preparation for and environment surrounding the drug use plays an important role in how well it works. His team would spend hours talking with people about their cancer and about what was going to happen when they took the drug. When some began to have a negative experience while under the influence, members of his team would offer reassurance or hold their hands to ground them. And with that grounding, the unease and fear would subside, leading them to a transcendent experience and an enduring reduction of their depression and anxiety.

The chants, songs, synchronous motions, and the like that traditionally accompany mystical techniques serve a purpose: they prepare our minds for the experience to come. They ease us into a state of calm and connection. But the vagal activity that underlies that state can come in other ways too. Patient, attentive, affirming conversations like those in Griffiths's experiments can also boost vagal tone. Is one method better than the other? That's a question scientists have yet to study. But I can already say with confidence that if we ignore the guiding hand that traditional rituals provide for seeking transcendence—whether we adopt them wholesale or accomplish the same biological and psychological effects via different methods—we might not only be losing out on better experiences; we might be playing with fire.

The Business of
Midlife I: Maintenance
for the Body

Everyone realizes that success and satisfaction in life depends a good deal on being mentally and physically healthy. A physical illness can limit our years; a mental one can trap us in despair. Religion should, and does, offer spiritual technologies that boost and repair our bodies and minds.

That many people turn to religion for healing is unlikely to surprise. For those afflicted with injury or disease, the idea of turning to God for comfort or cure is especially compelling. While 26 percent of people in the United States regularly pray to God to keep them healthy, that number rises dramatically when illness seems imminent. During the 2020 COVID-19 outbreak, the number of US adults praying for health and the end of the pandemic more than doubled to 55 percent. And a quarter of these people weren't even religious; they just started praying when the prospect of coming down with COVID made their mortality suddenly seem all too real.

When a health threat isn't just a distant possibility but a looming reality, the percentage of people who pray to God grows even more. Eighty-five percent of people who are in the midst of a health crisis like cancer report turning to prayer. But prayer isn't the only tool religion has to offer. They also provide rituals meant to heal the body and mind.

When it comes to improving health, religion works in two ways. The first is religion as vaccine. Vaccines work preventively; they stop a problem before it takes root. By boosting our immune response to influenza viruses, the flu vaccine protects our bodies from the annual viral assault. Regrettably, though, we can't always avoid illness or injury. Fortunately, religion also functions as a medicine. Unlike vaccines, medicines go to work once an illness hits. We take antibiotics to cure an infection or SSRIs to combat depression. As we'll see in this chapter, religious practices use both preventive and restorative means to protect our bodies and minds against the ravages of age, injury, and disease.

Before we examine how, I want to state two caveats. First, I won't be discussing religious biologics. By that, I mean I'll avoid talking about folk medicines or therapies. Many faiths have healing traditions, like Hinduism's Ayurveda or traditional Chinese medicine based on the cosmic dualism of yin and yang that focus on herbal or dietary cures. I'm not saying that such practices can't be effective. Some work well, some do nothing, and some do more harm than good. Any that are helpful will often be very narrow in their effects: a specific treatment for a specific ailment. For this reason, the study of biologics is best left to bioprospectors, since they likely work more through biochemistry, as drugs or nutrients do, rather than via a specific religious framing.

Second, I won't comment on the power of deities to heal directly. As a scientist, I can say there's no strong evidence for healing miracles. Proving faith-based cures work would require consistent and replicable examples among many people—the same standard we'd require to license the use of any new drug. To date, the evidence just isn't there. That said, many of us, including me, have seen remarkable instances of healing that are hard to explain from a strictly scientific perspective. So while I can't prove that miracles happen, neither can I prove that they don't happen. This question, like the question of whether God exists, is well outside the scope of this book.

In this chapter, I'll focus on the ways that religion can boost physical and mental well-being. Here, as with so much of what we've examined up to now, we'll see that religion's effects on belief and community play central roles.

Booster Shots

Measles. Pneumonia. Flu. They're all diseases we hope to avoid, and for which we have vaccines to protect us. As with any vaccine, though, the success rate won't be 100 percent. Still, vaccines do substantially reduce the odds that we'll succumb to a specific illness. Religion, as I've said, can work in a similar way—not by directly priming our immune system to fight a specific pathogen, but by boosting the body's and the mind's resilience so that they can better confront whatever health challenges come their way.

This doesn't mean that the link between religion and health is as straightforward as, say, the link between the smallpox vaccine and smallpox. Many factors can complicate the picture. The first has to do with timing. The statistics I cited show that many people turn to religion only when they're already sick, which removes any vaccine-like benefit religion might offer. Other people turn to religion later in life in an effort to find meaning or prepare their souls for a death that might come sooner than they'd like. Here, too, religion's ability to keep the body healthy is somewhat constrained; years have taken their toll without its buffering effect. And a body that hasn't already been strengthened by religious practice necessarily starts off in a weaker state when health challenges arise.

A second complication is that some religions—or smaller communities within them—frown on modern medicine. Some, like Christian Scientists, reject almost all medical treatment; others, like certain Orthodox Jews or members of the Dutch Reformed Church, avoid vaccinations. These theologically guided decisions will harm people's health.

Still, if it's true that, overall, religion can protect health, we should be able to find evidence of that effect, even when taking into account not only these complications but others having to do with income, access to medical care, and the like. Although the link between religion and health might be difficult to identify clearly in any single person, we should nonetheless be able to see the boost religion offers when we look across hundreds of people.

When the Pew Research Center examined many of the world's largest databases to study the links between religion and well-being, it found that more people in the United States who actively participated in their faiths reported better health than did those who were less engaged or entirely unaffiliated with a religion (32 percent versus 27 percent and 25 percent, respectively) even after controlling for a host of other demographic and economic factors. Citizens of Mexico and Taiwan showed a similar pattern. Yet even in countries where this link didn't appear quite as strong, people who actively engaged with their faiths tended to avoid certain health risks more than others did. For example, Pew observed a 5 percent reduction in the number who said they frequently drank alcohol and a 10 percent reduction in the number who said they regularly smoked—two behaviors strongly linked to impaired health.

Speaking as a psychologist, I can tell you that while people's self-reports are a valuable way to gather lots of data, they're also not necessarily accurate. It's not that most people lie but that they're not the best objective source of information about their own experiences. What one person thinks is good health, another might believe requires a visit to the doctor. We all have different thresholds for medical concern. For this reason, I think better information about the links between religion and health comes from studies that use more objective measures: blood pressure, cardiac function, mental health diagnoses, and death rates.

In 2001, the Mayo Clinic conducted a systematic review of hundreds of studies from the previous three decades that examined links between religion and health. Supporting my vaccine idea, a clear pattern emerged: the vast majority of studies found that people who regularly took part in religious activities were objectively healthier. To get a flavor, let's start with what is probably the broadest and most unambiguous measure of health: not dying. One major study that followed over five thousand people (aged twenty-one to sixty-five) for twenty-eight years showed that those who were active in their faiths were 23 percent less likely to die during this period than others were, even adjusting for factors such as age, body-mass index, baseline health, and education level. Another study that followed almost two thousand adults fifty-five and over found something quite similar: a 24 percent reduction in the mortality rate for the religiously active compared to inactive. In fact, when the Mayo Clinic looked across forty-two such studies, which in total examined over 126,000 people, religion provided an unmistakable benefit: those who actively participated had a 29 percent increased survival rate compared to others during the years they were followed.

Focusing our lens more narrowly, let's look first at cardiovascular disease. A study that followed ten thousand Israeli men showed that being part of an Orthodox community decreased the risk of a fatal heart attack by 20 percent compared to those who followed a more secular lifestyle, even when taking age, cholesterol levels, and related health considerations into account. In a similar vein, another study that followed almost four thousand adults sixty-five and older confirmed that those who were religiously active were 40 percent less likely to suffer from high blood pressure. Once again, these aren't cherry-picked findings. As the Mayo Clinic report makes clear, 75 percent of studies examining the effect of religiosity on heart health show a benefit, as do 87 percent of studies examining blood pressure.

When Mayo turned its attention to other objective measures of health, the results were the same. People who engaged more with the practices of their faith ate healthier foods, smoked less, had fewer hospitalizations, and, among those who were admitted, had shorter stays in the hospital. Taken together, these findings make clear that religiosity improves people's physical health.

Of course, good health doesn't only involve the body. The brain is also subject to malady. But like the body that carries it around, the brain also receives a health benefit from regularly taking part in religious activities. For example, a study of people aged fifty-five to eighty-nine found that being more engaged with religion not only reduced people's risk of becoming depressed but also shortened the time they needed to recover from a depressive episode if one did occur. And like the findings for physical health, there are many more studies to back this one up. Of twenty-nine studies the

Mayo Clinic examined that focused on religiosity and depression, twenty-four confirmed a benefit. Religion's effects on anxiety disorders show a similar pattern. A comprehensive review of nearly seventy studies, some of which are prospective and thus examined changes in people as their religiosity grew or waned, confirmed that regular participation in religious activities corresponds to decreased levels of anxiety.

Religion's benefits for psychological well-being aren't limited to preventing mood disorders. One of the most common problems that accompanies serious ongoing health crises like cancer or multiple sclerosis is the mental toll that comes from a newfound feeling of vulnerability. Not only can suffering from a chronic disease leave people struggling with pain, sadness, and fear, it can also lead to more existential concerns about the purpose of their lives. Religious practices have been shown to ease these existential woes that can plague the waking hours of people facing lengthy or even terminal ailments.

One prime example can be seen in people dealing with an advanced stage of cancer, who must daily confront both their mortality and the pain caused by their illness and treatment. Those who use positive religious coping strategies—like prayers focusing on God's love and a sense of connection to religious communities—report a better quality of life. Reading scripture, praying, and seeking pastoral counseling each play a role in helping people come to terms with their situations and reducing stress. If we look at other chronic illnesses, we find a similar pattern time and again.

How exactly does religion protect people's health? Here again, much of its influence comes via two routes: belief and community. In almost every study I described above, religion only offered a sizable benefit to people who actively took part in its practice. Checking a box on a survey to self-identify as Muslim, Jewish, Christian, or Buddhist does nothing to improve our health. These improvements come only from living a faith—regularly engaging in the practices and rituals that help our belief and sense of community grow.

To see how this works, let's start with belief. Many religions focus on healthy behaviors using the idea of the body as a temple. Many explicitly frown upon overindulgence in alcohol, tobacco, or recreational drugs. As you might then expect, it's true, as we saw above, that those who have stronger religious beliefs tend to smoke less, drink less, and avoid substance abuse. It's also true that greater religious engagement makes people more likely to see a physician for preventive care. In fact, Judaism's Talmud is explicit about this; it goes so far as to forbid people to live in towns where no physician is present.

The effect of belief isn't limited to narrow health-related rules, however. Basic belief in a deity also plays a role. As I mentioned in this book's introduction, religious faith leads to a calming sense of certainty in life that everything happens for a reason. This reduced stress, which corresponds to reduced strain on the cardiovascular and immune systems, is directly tied to better health. Simply put, if you believe that God loves you and has a plan for you, you'll feel less stress when facing an illness. If, however, you begin to question your faith—to feel that God has abandoned you—the exact opposite will happen: your quality of life will suffer. Here again is why actively taking part in religious services that emphasize God's love can foster well-being, even in times of crisis.

Taking part in religious practices also builds community. As we've seen, simply sitting in a room together doesn't do much to make people feel emotionally close. Religions aren't just a club; they work on the brain in deeper ways. Praying, singing, and moving together nudge the mind to create and strengthen social bonds.

It's the ways these rituals synchronize heartbeats, breathing rates, and bodily movements that create a sense of connection between people who might otherwise never interact beyond a quick hello. The feelings of gratitude and compassion that sermons and prayer evoke spill over in the moment to make listeners more willing to lend a hand to one another and start a relationship that otherwise might never have bloomed. Shared rituals provide the heat to break the ice or solder a social tie.

We've already seen how these practices can enhance bonding on a small scale, but when we're considering health issues, taking a broader view is helpful for understanding just how effective they can be. In surveying 2,500 US citizens across the age spectrum, the American Enterprise Institute found that belonging to a religious congregation reduced the percentage of people who reported feeling lonely at times from 45 percent to 35 percent. What's really interesting is how this pattern changes if you break it down by age. Millennials tend to be a bit lonelier than baby boomers. Some of this difference can be explained by the fact that this younger generation is less rooted to a geographic locale and less likely to be married. But religion also plays a role.

Millennials are less religiously active than boomers. And once you control for this difference, along with differences in marriage rates and geographic mobility, the disparity in loneliness between the two groups disappears. Put another way, religious activity is one of the three fundamental factors that determine whether a young person is likely to feel alone in the world. Whereas 35 percent of millennials who take part in religious services at least once a week report feeling lonely, that number rises to 50 percent among those who never attend.

Among the elderly—a time of life when loneliness can grow due to the passing of spouses and friends—taking part in religious activity builds a sense of connection. A large study by the National Social Life, Health, and Aging Project of US adults aged fifty-seven to eighty-five confirmed that regularly taking part in religious services helped them become part of communities and, as a result, feel less lonely.

When it comes to physical illness, social ties also play an important role. Loneliness contributes to a host of maladies, including viral illness, heart disease, diabetes, sleep disorders, hypertension, and depression. It follows that anything a person does to reduce loneliness should also improve their health. And as we've just seen, religious activity does just that.

There's one other easy way to see whether religious beliefs and communities sustain health: look at the people who live the longest. In 2005, National Geographic fellow Dan Buettner, working with a team of demographers, identified five communities across the globe where many people live to be one hundred or more. He labeled these places blue zones—a name that continues to be applied to locales where longevity is common. People living in these places eat a diet dominated by fresh fruits and vegetables. They get a lot of moderate exercise. And they don't drink or smoke heavily. But there are other reasons for their longevity too. One is family support. People residing in blue zones tend to have strong family connections, with different generations often living together in the same home. They also tend to be actively religious. By that, I don't mean that blue zoners are exceptionally pious. I mean that they regularly partake in the religious rituals and celebrations that unite their community.

The only blue zone in the United States—the large Seventh-day Adventist community in Loma Linda, California—offers a great example. Longevity there is partly due to pleasant weather year-round, making it easier to be active and outside. But that's true of many other towns and cities in the United States. The Adventists' religion certainly adds to their good health. Their beliefs lead them to avoid alcohol, tobacco, and recreational drugs, as well as to consume a plant-based diet. But the fact that many Adventists live in Loma Linda also gives them a strong sense of community. Their faith brings people together in a supportive network that reduces stress.

Still, it's hard to figure out how much influence each of these factors have when they all occur together. When trying to isolate the impact of religion alone, we can turn to another spot on the American map where church is embraced, but so, too, are pork sausages, lard, and meatballs, and where snow falls a good portion of the year: Roseto, Pennsylvania. Roseto is a small town in the Pocono Mountains where Italian immigrants settled during the first half of the twentieth century and carved out a tight-knit community for themselves. As is typical of Italian Americans—I know because I am one—family and Catholicism are as central a part of life as good food. But while the Rosetans were able to import the first two of these in their normal forms—the Catholic schools and church pews were full, as were their multifamily homes—the daily diet didn't quite follow the Mediterranean model. Olive oil was expensive, and the ideal season for fresh vegetables, let alone outdoor exercise, was shorter than in Italy. So the townsfolk made do with substitutions. They ate more meat, pasta, and cheese, and they fried their meat in lard instead of browning it in olive oil.

Despite that diet, physicians started noticing in the 1960s that, for some reason, Roseto's Italians suffered much lower rates of heart disease than people in neighboring towns—a fact that led medical researcher and new summer resident Dr. Stewart Wolf to take a more scientific look.

What Wolf found was startling. For most American men, the

risk of dying from heart disease increases with age, especially after fifty. But for the men of Roseto, the risk stayed near zero from ages fifty-five to sixty-four. And although it rose for those over sixty-five, it did so at half the national average. Try as he might, Wolf couldn't find any physical reason for the resilience of Rosetans' hearts. There was no beneficial genetic mutation. Their diets weren't any lower in saturated fat than were those of people in the surrounding towns. There was one big difference, though: the way Rosetans lived. As Wolf and his colleague John Bruhn observed, life in Roseto was defined by family and the church. Over 75 percent of the town was Roman Catholic. The Rosetans were so dedicated to their faith that they even built their own church when the local diocese refused to fund one. Outside the home, life in Roseto was defined by the rhythms of the local parish: weekly Mass, monthly festivals to honor the saints, charity drives, and church-directed social events.

Roseto isn't an official blue zone. And since the 1960s, life has begun to change there, with more city folk moving in for cheaper homes and younger Italian Americans moving away for better jobs. But the story of Roseto does offer a way to gauge how religion-induced social connection on its own affects health, apart from local environment and diet. In fact, at the end of their investigation, Wolf and Bruhn concluded that the Rosetans' Catholicism—precisely because of the ways it strengthened social bonds that reduced loneliness and stress—played a primary role in protecting their cardiovascular health. By regularly bringing people together, religion reduced loneliness and stress and all the cardiovascular problems they bring.

In mixed-faith or larger communities, what is known as the Roseto effect will be less prominent. People will be less likely to attend the same church or join the same clubs. But that doesn't mean religion's benefits are out of reach for non-Rosetans. Most churches, synagogues, mosques, and temples offer an open hand to anyone new to a community who is looking for company. But as societies turn away from them, this option fades. And with it fades an important tool for forming the bonds that sustain our minds and bodies.

Take Your Medicine

Prevention is a great strategy, but it can't completely protect us from injury and disease. When those challenges arise, religious rituals take on a therapeutic role, either by attempting to cure a person of a specific ailment or at least to reduce the pain it causes.

Healing rituals can be separated into two types: passive and active. As the name suggests, passive rituals don't require much of the sufferers. They just need to accept the healing power coming from others. Active rituals take the opposite approach. While a priest, shaman, or elder might be present to guide the rite, people hoping to be cured can't just sit quietly. They must actively engage in the process for it to work. Both types of rituals can be quite effective, but they rely on different mechanisms.

Let's start with the passive type. Across religions, many healing rites make use of touch and prayer, or what's known as a laying on of hands. In Christianity, where this practice is most developed, the power to heal is believed to be one of the gifts of the Holy Spirit. Those who possess this rare gift—and exactly who that is and whether it can include laypeople vary by denomination—are thought to be capable of curing physical and mental illnesses. At the start of these rituals, the healer prays for the power to channel God's healing energy. Next, they approach the sufferer and lay their hands upon the head or other afflicted areas. But while this core part of the ritual is constant, the context in which it occurs can take one of two forms.

In the traditional form, the entire ritual occurs quietly. A priest, minister, or other authorized member of the laity meets and prays with a person in need of healing. The healer then solemnly lays their hands upon the sufferer's head while continuing to pray. For example, in the Roman Catholic rite known as the anointing of the sick, a priest lays his hands on an ill person using *oleum infirmorum*—a sacred oil that traditionally consisted of pure olive oil that had been blessed. As the priest gently applies oil to the sufferer's forehead, he quietly intones, "Through this holy anointing, may the Lord in His love and mercy help you with the grace of the Holy Spirit." Next, massaging the oil into the sufferer's hand, he says "May the Lord who frees you from sin, save you and raise you up." In the past, this rite was often used only for people on their deathbeds, where it was known as the sacrament of extreme unction. Today, though, it's also used to give strength and fortitude to anyone combating an illness. In this case, the "raise you up" part of the ritual's last line refers to getting up from a bed or wheelchair, not a raising up to heaven after death.

The second way to conduct this ritual isn't nearly as quiet or solemn. Charismatic and Pentecostal Christians worship God differently than do their more traditional brethren. The difference between charismatic and Pentecostal movements is minor: the former remains under the umbrella of mainline churches, while the latter operates entirely on its own. Both are united by their belief in the importance of experiencing the Holy Spirit's power personally—an experience often brought about with boisterous singing, passionate preaching, and, in many congregations, speaking in tongues.

The "tongue" here refers to the language of the angels. It sounds a lot like human speech. It has a similar cadence. It uses familiar intonations and sounds. But the ways sounds are strung together don't produce any known words. So while speaking in tongues sounds like a foreign language, it's not one that any average person can translate. I say average because people can also be blessed with the gift of translation. Being able to speak in tongues marks someone as imbued with the power of the Holy Spirit—a belief that's especially important when the healer is a layperson, as it marks them, like clergy, as being favored by God.

In addition to being boisterous, the charismatic and Pentecostal laying on of hands usually takes place in packed church halls or auditoriums with fervent prayer and song echoing from the walls. Anyone who feels the need can approach the healer, and as they do so, a few people known as catchers will come up behind them. When the healer, who may be speaking in tongues, lays hands upon the afflicted, the emotional electricity in the air often leads them to cry, shake, or even faint. That's the reason for the catchers. Those who do faint will spend a time "resting in the spirit" before awakening to a new and, hopefully, improved state.

Whether they're quiet or loud, the focus of these rites is the same: a touch from a person favored by God to channel His healing power. For the recipient, it's about as close as they can come to feeling the hand of God in this life. And for that reason, it can be a very transformative event in psychological terms.

Belief in God can reduce stress, and reduced stress is good for the body. But that benefit accrues over time. The belief I'm talking about here is that one can heal rapidly: a belief in the method of healing itself. And putting debate of miracles aside, anytime people believe a treatment can heal, they have a formidable medicine on their side: the placebo effect.

By definition, a placebo is something that has no discernible biological effect; its ingredients are inert. To many people, the idea that a placebo can heal seems silly. But physicians have long used placebos as powerful tools. *A New Medical Dictionary*—an authoritative text published in London in 1785—describes placebo use as a common medical practice. In the early 1900s, Dr. Richard Clarke Cabot of Harvard Medical School stated that he and almost every physician he knew frequently gave their patients placebos in the form of bread pills. These doctors believed the fake pills helped patients because of those patients' expectations. And lest anyone think these doctors of old were ignorant or superstitious, modern science continues to prove that placebos work. They've been shown to produce clinically significant improvement in a wide range of maladies: chronic pain, anxiety, depression, Parkinson's disease, asthma, allergies, recovery from surgery, and deficiencies in the immune system. The placebo effect isn't a frivolous parlor trick; it's a partial solution to a problem, and one that religions have been using for millennia before modern medicine discovered its benefits.

Placebos can work in several different ways. The simplest is via confirmation bias. If you just took part in a healing ritual, you'd most likely be eager to see if it worked, meaning you'd be especially likely to notice any sign of improvement. In a nutshell, that's how confirmation bias works. When we look for facts that can confirm a prediction, our minds tend to ignore signs that don't. Our brains don't process information objectively. They direct our attention to what we're looking for and screen out much of the rest as noise. The result can be a biased view of the facts. But if that were all there was to placebo effects, they really wouldn't be very strong; the influence of confirmation bias would wear off as conflicting evidence mounted. But placebo effects work in several other ways too.

The predictions your brain makes can actually shape your reality, to a degree. They don't just tell you what to look for; they can change how you experience the world around you. Let's take pain as an example. Over time, most of us learn that medicines make us feel better. So when we take aspirin, we expect our pain to decrease. By observing the results from taking aspirin many times, our mind constructs a sensible belief that aspirin works.

Work by a team of scientists from the University of Maryland shows just how powerful predictions like this can be. On a post-surgical ward, the team set up a system where some patients received painkillers the usual way: a nurse would inject it into their IV lines. Others had it delivered at undisclosed times by a hidden pump connected to their IVs. Same drug; same types of surgeries. The only difference was that some of the people had the cue of seeing the medicine being administered. If that cue, and the expectation to which it gave rise, didn't matter, then both types of patients—those who knew they were getting the drug and those who didn't know—should have experienced the same degree of pain relief. But that's not what happened. Patients who didn't see the nurse injecting the painkiller into their IV lines needed much bigger doses to achieve the same degree of pain reduction as those who did. Now, this wasn't exactly a placebo effect, as the pain medicines were real in both cases, but it shows the power of "seeing is believing" when it comes to getting medicine.

On the other hand, fake surgeries—where doctors make incisions but then don't do anything else—are placebos in the truest sense of the word. To get approved, studies that compare fake surgery to true surgery tend to be focused on more minor ailments, such as acid reflux. It wouldn't be ethically appropriate to delay treatment for more serious conditions, even with a person's consent. Still, they offer a very powerful way to study how placebos work. For patients, being wheeled into an operating room and waking to the sight of a surgical incision in their skin are among the clearest signs there are of medical intervention. Amazingly, a review of placebo surgery studies found that 74 percent of people who had fake surgeries had a reduction in troublesome symptoms. And of those who reported a benefit, almost half rated the improvement in their symptoms to be equal to the amount of improvement reported by others who actually had real surgery to cure their ailments.

Belief is so powerful that its effects can even be measured within the brain itself. In other work, the University of Maryland team found that neurons in the brains of Parkinson's patients continue to respond to a placebo in the same ways they do to a true Parkinson's drug when a fake pill replaces it. Because it expects to function better, the brain actually makes itself do so.

Beliefs don't operate in a vacuum, though; they have a social aspect too. As we've seen, beliefs can be contagious—caught from or reinforced by the beliefs of others around us. And since placebos are based on belief, their effect is modulated by how much others believe in them. One of the best examples of this social sensitivity comes from an experiment in which people were randomly assigned to play the role of doctor or patient in a scenario meant to test how well two medical ointments controlled pain. In actuality, the ointments weren't medicinal at all; they were petroleum jelly. But in order to see how one person's beliefs about a placebo's effectiveness can influence another's, researchers first had to convince the "doctor" that thermedol—the name of the placebo ointment—worked better than the other ointment.

Making the doctor believe this fact required some clever sleight of hand using a medical device that could produce painful (but not harmful) amounts of heat when applied to the skin. Although the researchers told the doctors that the heat output was the same on every trial, they actually applied a lower intensity to skin that they had treated with thermedol than with the other ointment. As they hoped, the doctors reported feeling less pain from the probe placed on their own skin rubbed with thermedol—an experience that translated into a strong belief that thermedol was a superior pain medication.

Next, the researchers told the doctors that they'd be applying the two different ointments to patients' skin before conducting a similar test with them. The most interesting part of the experiments, though, was that the doctors weren't supposed to tell the patients anything about which of the ointments they believed would work better. When the doctors did place the heat probe on patients' skin, it always delivered the same amount of heat. But here's where the social power of belief became astoundingly apparent. Even though the level of heat and the two medicines used were objectively the same, the patients reported less pain when the thermedol was applied—exactly the condition in which the doctor, who was sitting across from them, expected less pain to occur. What's more, this wasn't simply patients somehow sensing they were supposed to erroneously report less pain. Their physiological states differed, too, indicating that they actually felt less pain when they used the placebo ointment than when they didn't.

It's clear from this finding, which the team has replicated, that patients were somehow picking up on doctors' beliefs about how well each treatment would work. In fact, patients reported that their doctors seemed more caring when they were applying the thermedol, which would be expected since the doctors actually believed it was better at reducing pain. The message here is powerful: the more confidence a healer has in a treatment, the more effective it will be, even if it's a placebo.

Healing rites make good use of all these psychological mechanisms. Through prayer, holy oil, singing, etc., they focus people's attention on the ritual laying on of hands. Much like a fake surgical scar, people can't miss it or forget it. The memory is strengthened because it's multisensory—sight, sound, smell, and touch are all involved.

These rituals also give healers an aura of expertise. They've been marked by God as special—a status reinforced by symbolic clothing or the respect others show them. And as we saw in chapter 2, perceived expertise goes a long way toward enhancing belief. What's more, unlike physicians who might knowingly use a placebo to help a patient, religious healers truly believe these rites have power. This, too, enhances their effect. By combining all these elements together, healing rituals are an immensely useful technology.

What I find most fascinating is that belief in the placebo effect itself—believing that a pill you know to be fake will still heal you—works the same way. While it may seem incredibly hard to believe, emerging research using open-label placebos—medicines clearly labeled as inert for all to see—shows that they can have the same beneficial effects as their counterfeit cousins.

Early evidence for this comes from a study on irritable bowel syndrome (IBS) in which some patients took a capsule that they were told contained only an inert filler. Though they knew the pills had no therapeutic ingredients, those who took them twice daily for two weeks following a doctor's instructions reported a significant reduction in IBS symptoms. Open-label trials have also shown success with medical problems ranging from attention deficit hyperactivity disorder (ADHD), to migraines, to back pain.

No one is quite sure how and why they work. But what's becoming evident is that three ingredients are necessary. First, a person has to trust their health provider. If they don't see the provider as caring and competent, the placebo has little effect. Second, there must be a ritual. The provider can't simply say, "You're healed. Next patient." They need to offer a pill or cream, touch the painful area, or otherwise act in a way that suggests healing is underway. Third, a person needs to believe in the power of the placebo effect; they need to expect that taking a placebo can help.

When all these factors are present, the mind can work its magic on the body. As research by a team of psychologists at Stanford University showed, this combination can even reduce the severity of an allergic reaction. When the team injected a histamine solution under people's skins—a safe way to generate hives, which are typical of an allergic reaction—they found that people's belief in the power of placebo effects, when combined with these other ingredients, reduced the severity of the response. Those who felt comfortable with the doctor who applied a placebo cream to the injection site—a cream that the doctor told them was completely inert—showed less of a skin reaction if they also believed in the placebo effect.

Open-label placebos aren't that different from the closed-label type found in many healing rituals. In religious rites, both the healer and the sufferer believe the ritual has the power to heal. The same goes for open-label placebos. It's just that here, beliefs about healing aren't based on religion; they're based on science. If we believe that science proves placebos can heal, then taking one is likely to help us. But that belief isn't sufficient to work on its own. We need a provider we trust to tell us a placebo will work, and, most important, we need a ritual. We need to do something—take a pill, use a cream, touch spots on our bodies—for our minds to buy it deep down. And when that *something* is embedded in a rich context of prayer and symbols, it becomes even more convincing. That's the genius of religion. Centuries ago, across different continents, in eras without the amazing medical technologies we have at our disposal today, religions figured out a formula to help people heal themselves—a formula we're only now rediscovering.

Before we move on, I want to make one thing clear. While

placebo effects are real, they're usually not the best way to deal with medical problems. They can help with ailments for which the body holds the potential to heal itself. The brain can produce its own endorphins to combat pain. The body can modulate its own stress and immune responses. But when it comes to excising a tumor, repairing a compound fracture, and the like, placebos won't help much. So I'm not advocating that people turn to placebo-based treatments over more medically viable ones. What I am saying is that we should certainly consider placebos one of the many technologies we can use to heal.

Given the power of placebos, I'd urge you to experiment with creating your own healing rituals of the passive type with family or friends. Just make sure they follow the general framework. Talk about the scientifically proven efficacy of placebos, and how laying hands on an achy head or rumbly belly can work similarly. Make a true ritual out of it. Quietly sing a soothing song or move your hand gently and rhythmically. Wrap someone who's feeling under the weather in a "magic" blanket in a very intentional way. The keys are to show compassion, to employ a ritual, and to help each other believe it can make a difference. Because it can.

God Helps Those Who Help Themselves

Up to now, I've focused on rituals that don't require much effort from sufferers. But just as some types of modern healing require people to work for a cure—undertaking difficult physical therapy to relearn how to walk, resisting and overcoming unhealthy urges to beat addiction—so, too, do some spiritual technologies. And while they're not easy, these practices can offer powerful healing to those willing to put in the work or make the necessary sacrifices.

Buddhist meditation is a prime example. Although it can seem passive to the casual observer, for the sitter, there's a lot of mental struggle going on to tame the mind. If you ask any Buddhist teacher why meditation was developed, you'll get a straightforward answer: to reduce suffering. Yet that seemingly simple response masks a good deal of complexity. Suffering can take many forms: pain from bodily ills, distress from unfulfilled desires, depression from separation and disconnection, and the like. Over the past decade, science is beginning to find that, in ways large and small, there's truth to the Buddhist belief: meditation can help with each of these. For now, though, let's focus on bodily ills.

Although there are many forms of meditation, most emphasize developing a state of mindful acceptance. By focusing on their breath, scanning their bodies for sensations, and pulling back their wandering minds, people begin to free themselves from the ego and its endless attempts to control their environs. They stop worrying about all the what-ifs and begin living more in the present. The result is less stress, anxiety, depression, and inflammation.

To me, one of the best examples of the power of mindfulness to reduce physical suffering comes from research conducted by Yale neuroscientist Hedy Kober. I say best not because it shows the most dramatic effect—many other studies show a strong association between meditation and more severe health problems—but because it lets us see how mindfulness alters the brain's response to pain in real time.

After spending thirty minutes training people in techniques of mindful acceptance, Kober had them recline in an MRI scanner. During the next thirty minutes, she alternated between showing them pleasant and horrific images while also between applying pleasantly warm (approximately 105 degrees Fahrenheit) and painfully hot (approximately 118 degrees Fahrenheit) probes to their skin. It sounds a bit like a modern-day torture chamber, but these were all consenting participants with safety protocols in place to ensure the heat probe wouldn't damage their skin. While they were inside the MRI machines, Kober told people at specific times to use the techniques they had just learned.

The prediction was straightforward: people should feel less emotional distress, both in response to negative images and hot skin probes, when they were using the mindfulness techniques. The great thing about this study was it didn't rely solely on people's self-reports. That's an important detail because people might have felt pressure to temper their verbal ratings of discomfort when they were told to use the techniques. To get around that problem, Kober scanned their brains. That's why they were inside the MRI tube.

As she expected, Kober found that when people used techniques for mindful acceptance, activity in brain areas associated with negative emotions and pain significantly quieted. This tells us that her participants were responding accurately when they reported feeling less distress. While in this state of acceptance, their brains actually registered less discomfort as they saw horrific images or had a hot probe placed on their skin.

Kober's study only involved one half-hour lesson in mindful acceptance. That effort pales in comparison to what would occur over months or years of meditation training. And so, too, would its effects on the brain. Still, her finding shows how much a short, simplified version of Buddhist meditation can influence how people respond to pain.

These active spiritual technologies can work for serious mental anguish as well. I've already mentioned how meditation can aid depression and anxiety, but there are many other types of psychological maladies. Post-traumatic stress disorder (PTSD) is one that can be especially debilitating. But an ancient spiritual technology is showing promise as a therapy.

As its name suggests, PTSD arises from exposure to a traumatic event—one that often involves serious injury, abuse, or even the deaths of other people. And while anyone can be afflicted with it, PTSD often strikes soldiers because of their proximity to these horrors. Whatever its source, the burdens people with PTSD carry are excruciating. Without warning, memories of the trauma burst into their minds, sometimes so vividly as to make them tremble, cry, or even run in fear. As a result, those with PTSD frequently abuse alcohol and opioids in an attempt to allay their symptoms.

War and trauma aren't new scourges. Like disease, they've regrettably been with us for as far back in time as we can peer. For that reason, religions have developed effective technologies to help heal the pain they cause. One of the more intriguing is the Native American sweat. For centuries, it's been used to help Native American warriors recover from the horrors of combat. And today, many US soldiers, with the blessing of the US Department of Veterans Affairs, have begun using it for the same purpose.

Although the specifics of the ritual can vary across tribes, the basic form is fairly standard. The first thing you need is a sweat lodge. Many Native American tribes use the pliable branches of willow trees to construct a dome-shaped structure for the lodge, with the doorway usually facing east toward the rising sun. Next, the builders cover the willow skeleton with blankets, skins, or other insulating materials. While lodge size can vary, they typically hold anywhere from six to eighteen people. But whatever the size, lodges are built with a depression at the center to hold heated stones. When it's time for the ritual, the leader lights a fire outside the lodge and places stones, usually about a foot or so in diameter, into this pit.

When the time is right, the medicine man or other elder leads participants in prayers, chants, and drumming. He then invites them into the lodge, where they sit around the central pit. As they wait, others carefully bring hot stones from the fire outside into the lodge and place them in the pit. When enough stones arrive, the medicine man douses them with water containing medicinal herbs. The steam rises, as does the temperature. And when the flap to the outer world is closed, everything becomes pitch-black.

The specifics of what happens inside the lodge are well guarded. But in general, most ceremonies involve four cycles of sweating, with the lodge flap being opened between each. During the sweats, people endure temperatures well over 100 degrees Fahrenheit while sitting in darkness. Some describe the feeling as womb-like; others as disorienting. But however they describe it, all agree it's an uncomfortable trial. While they sweat, the ritual leader encourages people to express what they feel when the spirit moves them. Some weep, some moan, some rock as they release feelings, fears, or regrets that they've pent up—albatrosses that fly away as cool air rushes in when the flap is raised.

In an interview with Voice of America, Craig Falcon, a member of the Blackfeet tribe who leads sweats for veterans, described the experience like this: "You come back from war with things attached to you. And some of those things may not be good. They could be memories. Or it could be somebody you killed, and that person attaches himself to you and comes home with you. Ceremonies help wash those things off, send them back to where they came from and get you back to who you are."

While there aren't yet any official statistics about the benefits of sweat rituals, more than a thousand veterans who have suffered with PTSD have already taken part in them. Their experiences have been so positive that more Veterans Administration hospitals in the Northwest have decided to build lodges on their grounds.

Sweats offer peace and a community of support. At a psychological level, the heat and darkness that envelops people creates a sense of spatial disorientation. There's nothing on which people can focus their attention, and so that attention turns inward. The darkness also creates a sense of anonymity that can encourage people to express their sorrows and fears while building a bond among participants who face the oppressive heat together. Everyone empathically accepts whatever others reveal, building a strong sense of brotherhood. And when the flap is finally opened, the cooling breezes that wash the problem-laden steam away offer a sense of relief and renewal.

This ancient ritual somewhat resembles one of the more successful modern therapies for PTSD. This treatment, known as prolonged exposure therapy, encourages people to repeatedly recall and retell the story of their traumatic events in an environment where they feel safe. The guiding principle is that by doing so, they'll eventually become better able to process the trauma and eventually let it go. To me, it seems that the Native American shamans figured out a similar formula hundreds of years ago—one that future research might reveal to work even better.

For all their benefits, we must keep in mind that these healing rituals are complex. Sweats differ from the laying on of hands, and both differ greatly from meditation. If not handled correctly, their power might generate problems rather than cures. For example, although meditation is often beneficial, we've already seen it can lead to psychological disturbance in some people. Similar cautions apply to sweat lodges. Deaths have occurred when people who haven't been trained in the ancient techniques for managing heat exposure and stress try to conduct the ritual. So while we can try to create new rituals or modify existing ones, we do so at some peril if we stray too far from well-honed techniques.

This doesn't mean that healing rituals can't be used in a secular context if we pay attention to and honor the ancient wisdom at their roots. There's already evidence for this view. Many Americans who meditate do so without attaching any religious doctrine to it. The last time I heard the Dalai Lama speak at a conference, he explicitly stated that people don't need to become Buddhists in order to reap meditation's benefits. Those who are interested are free to study and debate Buddhist doctrine about reincarnation and the like. But none of that is necessary to meditate. Whether in person or by book or app, the only thing that's required is finding a knowledgeable and experienced teacher to guide you. And that's a rule to live by, whatever new healing ritual you might be looking to undertake.

6

The Business of Midlife II: Maintenance for the Soul

"To everything there is a season, a time for every purpose under heaven." So begins a famous passage from the Book of Ecclesiastes from the Judeo-Christian scriptures. There's a time to laugh, a time to weep, a time to dance, and a time to build. But the scriptures are vague regarding when those seasons should actually occur. Sometimes the answer is clear. The moment you have a child, or when you lose someone you love. But more often than not, the answer isn't obvious.

Hinduism is rare in offering a lifelong schedule of sorts. Dating from before 500 BCE, the Hindu Vedas suggest that the path of life should comprise four distinct sections known as ashramas. The first, brahmacharya, is the time for learning. From birth to young adulthood, people should focus on acquiring an education and preparing for a profession. The second ashrama, grihastha, begins at twenty-five and is the time to focus on family and professional advancement. It centers on worldly goals: wealth, status, and sexual pleasure. At around fifty, people are supposed to transition to vanaprastha—a time to turn away from professional ambition, raising children, and material pleasures, and focus on wisdom, spirituality, and service. If the transition to vanaprastha is successful, and for many it can be a difficult one, a person will be well prepared for life's final phase, sannyasa. Here they're encouraged to devote themselves completely to the divine in preparation for death and moksha—final liberation from the cycle of rebirth.

Putting theological questions of reincarnation aside, the first three phases of the ashramas are as relevant to life today as they were thousands of years ago. But it's vanaprastha—that last change needed of the first three phases, and as the laws of Manu note, when people's skin begins to wrinkle and their hair turns gray—that I want to focus on here. As we saw in the previous chapter, midlife is a time for change. But it's more gradual than puberty or marriage. The changes sneak up on us. Our health might slowly decline. Our hair might slowly gray. But midlife changes aren't limited to the physical. People's social lives change too. During midlife, the generation above you is starting to pass on, and the generation below you is starting to move out. As a result, it becomes difficult to ignore concerns about your own mortality and the loss of connection with loved ones. Add to this fact that in the modern world, many who are continuing to pursue a career during midlife are also beginning to feel burned-out or less satisfied with their professional pursuits, and you've got something of a perfect storm bearing down on people's happiness.

Data from across the world shows the effects of that storm. Wherever you look, people's happiness across the life span follows a U-shaped curve, with its nadir occurring right around age fifty. Happiness starts to decline in the late thirties and early forties, bottoming out between the late forties and early fifties, before beginning to rise again from the late fifties into the seventies and eighties. At that point, people's happiness tracks show a good deal of variability that depends on whether and when serious health issues arise. A similar pattern is revealed by antidepressant use. Data from twenty-seven European nations documenting the consumption of these drugs shows an inverted-U pattern across the same ages. Antidepressant use starts increasing in the mid-twenties, peaks in the late forties, and then drops through the sixties and seventies. In fact, the data make clear that people are three times more likely to take antidepressants around the age of fifty than around the ages of twenty or eighty.

One major reason behind this midlife drop in happiness is that most of us don't make the switch into a vanaprastha-like mindset when we should. And while this is true the world over, it's especially so in more modern, Western societies as the antidepressant data makes clear. When we delay turning our focus more toward virtues like kindness, generosity, service, and forgiveness—ones that help us find purpose and connection—we delay embracing values and behaviors that naturally sustain us as we age. In his book, *The Second Mountain*, David Brooks describes the importance of making that change this way: "If the first mountain is about building up the ego and defining the self, the second mountain is about shedding the ego and losing the self. If the first mountain is about acquisition, the second mountain is about contribution. . . . On the first mountain you tend to be ambitious, strategic, and independent. On the second mountain you tend to be relational, intimate, and relentless." The two different mountains refer, of course, to two different phases of life. Science supports

Brooks's argument that making that switch at the right time leads to greater well-being as people move through midlife.

Two psychological factors help people make this switch. A growing recognition of their impending mortality provides the motivation, and technologies that nudge them toward compassion, generosity, and forgiveness provide the tools. For religions, this translates into rituals that focus on the inevitability of death and the need for atonement.

If that's the case, it might seem a bit odd at first that most religions don't have specific rituals targeted to meet these goals. But on further thought, I think the reason why becomes clear. Since there's no one age at which these virtues aren't beneficial, ritualistically focusing on them solely at midlife would be a mistake. That's why rituals and practices that emphasize reminders of mortality and the need for kindness—things like Judaism's Yom Kippur, Christianity's Ash Wednesday, and Buddhist meditations on impermanence and loving-kindness—occur throughout life. But it's also true that the mind's interest in these rituals grows rapidly at midlife and continues in the years that follow. So there's no need to create a specific ritual for midlife because the mind naturally gravitates toward the appropriate rituals on its own.

For example, although the emphasis Jews place on most religious holidays remains fairly constant over the life span, it does change dramatically for two of them. While 37 percent of eighteen- to thirty-nine-year-olds believe that Yom Kippur—the Day of Atonement—is the most important holiday of the Jewish year, 20 percent view Hanukkah as such. But among Jews over sixty, the percentages change to 53 percent versus 6 percent. Put a different way, although Yom Kippur is seen as the holiest day of the liturgical year by the majority of Jews, for the young, the focus on gifts and pleasure is also relatively high. But as people age, their focus turns away from immediate pleasures and toward contemplating how best to live during the time that remains—a major focus of Yom Kippur.

We see a similar pattern when it comes to taking up meditation: the percentage of those who regularly meditate steadily climbs with age. Whereas 29 percent of people eighteen to twenty-nine meditate, the number rises to 44 percent among those fifty to sixty-four, and to 53 percent of those over sixty-five. It's not the young hipsters who most turn to mindfulness; it's older people seeking peace, joy, and meaning in the time they have left.

Dust to Dust

Every year, on the forty-sixth day before Easter Sunday, Catholics around the world solemnly line up to approach the priest presiding over Ash Wednesday services. As he turns to each, the priest dips his fingers in ash before tracing the symbol of the cross on their forehead. As he applies the black mark, he looks them in the eye while saying: "Remember you are dust, and unto dust you shall return." There's nothing subtle about Ash Wednesday. It's a blunt reminder that no matter who you are or what you have achieved, death awaits you. And for the middle-aged—those for whom death suddenly doesn't seem quite as remote and inconceivable as it once did—this stark reminder can pack a punch.

Like Ash Wednesday, the Jewish Days of Awe—the high holy days from Rosh Hashanah to Yom Kippur—also serve up a reminder of mortality. Symbolically, the Days of Awe represent the cycle of life. They begin on Rosh Hashanah with a celebration of the creation of humankind, and end on Yom Kippur with reminders of inescapable death. On the last day, many Jews customarily wear white as a reminder of the ivory-toned shrouds in which they will be buried. They forsake the needs of the body by abstaining from food, drink, and sex, thereby symbolically freeing themselves from their corporeal vehicle. Through Torah readings and personal reflection and prayer, the day's services emphasize repentance.

For Jews, the process of repentance, or *teshubah*, is fairly formalized and demanding. To be forgiven, you must not only regret a transgression but also resolve not to commit it again and confess it before God. Yom Kippur helps this process along by requiring Jews to recite the viddui nine times as part of the holy day's separate services. The viddui, which is also known as the Jewish deathbed confessional, is chanted in the first-person plural. Most of its many lines begin "We have . . . ," followed by a litany of sins: We have lied; We have stolen; We have caused grief; We have harmed others; We have . . . As people communally utter each sin, they gently beat their chests, both as a sign of ownership of the transgression and as a sign of punishment. Somewhat surprisingly, the melody of the chant isn't a solemn one; it's uplifting. But that actually fits with Yom Kippur's purpose: to make people feel empowered to change their ways rather than remain in the morass of their sins.

While admitting transgressions and seeking forgiveness for committing them is always noble, it's not always easy. And so, in addition to the viddui, Yom Kippur services add an additional psychological nudge. As the congregation recites the *Unetanneh Tokef*—one of the principal prayers said on Yom Kippur—people can't help but face the fact that they don't know how much time they have left to make amends. As they chant "Who will live and who will die? Who will die at their predestined time and who before their time? Who by water and who by fire, who by sword, who by beast, who by famine, who by thirst, who by storm, [and] who by plague?" the possibility that any among them might pass during the coming year is difficult to deny.

While holy days like Ash Wednesday and Yom Kippur emphasize our mortality, their impact, though powerful and important, is restricted to certain times of the year. That's why many faiths also regularly use less elaborate tools to remind us that our time is limited. In *The Imitation of Christ*, one of Christianity's most enduring and popular devotional tomes, the medieval religious scholar Thomas à Kempis points out how focusing on death can improve life. He explicitly urges Christians to meditate on death every day and in so doing, to recognize that they should live their lives as though they might be dead by nightfall. In a similar vein, Saint Ignatius of Loyola, founder of the Jesuit order, included meditations on death in the spiritual exercises he created. He recommended, for example, that people seeking spiritual growth should contemplate this question: If you were on your deathbed looking back on your life, what decisions do you wish you had made?

While these Judeo-Christian techniques certainly show convergence in their focus on death's inescapability, Buddhism also offers a set of tools. While there are many different forms of Buddhist meditation, as we've seen, they all share the goal of fostering a liberating sense of emptiness and nonself. Delving deeply into the theology behind these concepts would require a book in itself, but for our purposes here we need only note that one of the faith's central messages is that things in the world—including people—do not contain unique essences. One major reason we suffer in life is that our untrained minds disagree.

We all regularly categorize people and objects in certain ways and, as a result, we create attachments to them that often cause anxiety, pain, craving, and the like. Meditation seeks to break through those delusions about who we are and our place in the world. Everything is impermanent. And while this is not the place to debate the validity of Buddhist doctrine, there is a point to the practice that is highly relevant to the issues we're currently considering. As the revered Buddhist teacher Atisha suggested three thousand years ago, an awareness of death is necessary for meditation to accomplish its goals. Until and unless we accept that death is a normal part of life—that our bodies will ultimately fail—we'll persist in denial of the possibility or terror of its eventuality.

For this reason, many meditative techniques aim to help people become more mindful of death and impermanence, creating a sense of shortened time that pushes people toward less materialistic concerns. In fact, the Buddhists have developed a specific set of practices that explicitly focus on the awareness of death, some of which can be quite intense. In one, meditators sit next to decaying corpses or skeletons for weeks while contemplating that they, too, will share that fate. By watching the corpses decay while training their minds to accept rather than recoil from this macabre show, people come to accept openly and fearlessly our common fate.

Fortunately, Buddhism also offers less extreme techniques for accepting death. One of the most common uses the Nine Contemplations of Atisha. As part of this practice, Buddhists focus on nine "truths"—which include the fact that everyone will die, that everyone's life span is continuously decreasing, that death will come whether or not they're ready, that people's loved ones cannot save them from death, and that the human body is fragile and vulnerable.

I know, this doesn't sound cheery. But highlighting the inevitability of death serves a positive purpose, especially at midlife. Laura Carstensen, who directs the Stanford Center on Longevity, argues that what she calls time horizons across the life span— the time we feel we have left to live—play a central role in our motivations. When we perceive time to be open-ended—when death feels almost infinitely remote—we want to acquire knowledge and skills. We value novelty. We're looking to develop our careers, our wealth, and our status. But when time feels limited— when death suddenly seems an approaching possibility—our motivations shift. We come to value the familiar, the people and relationships that we already know make us happiest, and the activities that we've found to be emotionally meaningful. Put simply, as we feel the time slipping away, we want to fill what's left with joy, connection, and purpose.

Carstensen and her colleagues have found this pattern time and again in their research. But, to me, what truly proves her theory's validity is that it isn't tied solely to age. Her data shows that although most people start perceiving a shortened time horizon to death at around sixty years of age, the move toward or away from deeper connection and well-being can happen at any age if time horizons suddenly change in unexpected ways.

Epidemics offer a lens to study this idea. When disease is rampant, feelings of vulnerability to death quickly rise. For example, during the 2003 SARS outbreak in Hong Kong, young people suddenly felt more vulnerable. Like the elderly, they weren't sure how much time they might have left to live given the virus's rampage. As a result, their values suddenly changed to more closely mirror those held by people over sixty. Researchers found that the young's typical focus on personal advancement disappeared, replaced by a desire to seek fulfillment and contentment from deeper social connections and time spent on more socially meaningful pursuits. Motivation can move in the opposite direction too. As one example, when Carstensen's team asked older people to imagine what they would do if a new medical advance arrived that would allow them to live much longer than they'd expected, their values shifted toward those of the young. They wanted to spend more time learn-ing new skills and experiencing novelty.

These findings are important for two reasons. First, they offer proof that people's motivations don't change just because they reach a specific age. While the shift tends to happen around sixty, it can happen at any point across the life span. What drives it is the sense that time horizons are shortening. It's this flexibility, I believe, that offers people a chance to avoid the drop in happiness that typically occurs ten years earlier.

Imagine if we all made this transition in values by fifty instead of sixty—at the time the Hindu ashramas suggest we should. We know that people sixty to eighty tend to be much happier than their middle-aged counterparts. We also know that they place a greater emphasis on finding joy in connection with and service to other people than through individualistic or materialistic pursuits. By re-alizing and accepting that death is inescapable, they reorient their ways of living. But before I strongly recommend that fifty-year-olds adopt a different emphasis in their search for happiness—one based on connection and service rather than on more individual-istic pursuits—I'd need to know if there's any evidence that mak-ing this change *can* work earlier in life. At midlife, as opposed to retirement. Fortunately, there is some.

When psychologists compare how Americans and East Asians pursue happiness, they typically find that Americans favor a more individualistic route. For example, when Americans want to be happier, they buy something or try to learn a new skill. East Asians spend more time with friends and family or pursuing activities that benefit the community, like volunteering for a charity or helping elderly neighbors. The data shows that only one of these strategies works. In the United States, the more people seek happiness by fo-cusing on their own desires and pursuits, the less satisfied with life they end up feeling. But when East Asians pursue happiness their way—through social connection and service—they find it.

While following this advice can boost happiness at any point in life, it will be most helpful precisely at the time when, societally speaking, we're most unhappy: the time when midlife crises hit and we need to figure out what changes will make the remainder of our years more rewarding.

Each of the practices and rituals I described above, and others like them, can accomplish these goals in a much more powerful way than do simple reminders of death used in psychological research. So when experiments show that asking people what they'd like to do if they had only six months to live leads them to favor emotionally and socially meaningful activities, imagine how much more powerful religious rituals can be. The tactics used in experiments like these take place in bland, sterile environments. They don't speak to our minds through multiple channels. They don't evoke strong feelings through song, imagery, or intense contemplation. That's the province of religious rituals, which offers one reason why these practices can have a much more profound and lasting effect.

As I said before, accepting that death can come sooner than we might hope drives us to make the changes that bring lasting happiness. Rituals that emphasize it aren't meant just to shake the mind free from its illusions about immortality; they're designed, as we'll see next, also to convince us that fulfillment comes from connection and service. These advantages don't depend on a good job, physical strength, or social status—all things that become more tenuous as we age. They're sources of happiness that are available to us until we draw our last breath. In using or adapting the tools these rituals offer, we'll push ourselves to change how we pursue happiness earlier—say, by fifty rather than sixty—and avoid a decade or more of unhappiness and future regret about wasted time.

Fixing the Soul

We return now to the Jewish High Holy Days because they do a particularly good job of working the psychological levers that make us think about and, more important, act upon the values that most reliably produce happiness. During this ten-day stretch, believers enter a kind of psychic hothouse where they not only confront death's proximity but their own behaviors that prevent them from experiencing happiness.

The Talmud describes three heavenly books. On Rosh Hashanah, God writes the names of the righteous in the Book of Life. The names of the wicked He writes in the Book of Death. The names of those who have sinned but are not beyond hope (i.e., most of us) land in a third book. God suspends judgment on these people until Yom Kippur, meaning that during the days following Rosh Hashanah, their fates hang in the balance. If they prove their worth before the Day of Atonement, as Yom Kippur is known, their names will be moved to the Book of Life. If not, then they're consigned to the Book of Death. Either way, their fates are sealed for the coming year.

To help people make the right choices—to move them toward virtues like kindness, generosity, and forgiveness—these ten days focus on themes of *teshubah* (repentance and forgiveness) and *tzadakah* (good deeds and charitable donations). So during this time, Jews are called upon to act charitably while also being forced to remember their misdeeds and seek forgiveness. One way they do this, as we've seen, is by ritualistically reciting the viddui. More importantly, they must make amends directly with those they've harmed. In Judaism, praying to God isn't enough to be forgiven for harms you caused to others; those require you to seek forgiveness directly from the victims. That's the best way to repair relationships in this world.

By combining a sense of dwindling time with a strong nudge to do what's right—to help others, to be fair, to make peace—the Jewish High Holy Days prod people toward actions and values that will bring them lasting happiness. And for those at midlife—a time when concern with these rituals grows—this effect promises to be especially powerful.

While there's no research that directly examines the effects of rituals like these, there's good reason to think that having people reflect on their sins can actually change their behavior for the better. This might sound unlikely, especially given our earlier discussion of cognitive dissonance. From that perspective, making people realize that they've lied or cheated could lead them to accept the belief that they're selfish at heart. After all, one way to bring your beliefs about yourself and your behaviors into agreement is to alter your beliefs to match your behavior. But there are other factors to consider here: no one wants to think of themselves as selfish or immoral, and most sins aren't committed publicly. So unlike the situation where people are trying to figure out whether they believe in God—a situation where the best option isn't always clear—there's an obviously desirable outcome here: people want to see themselves as good. That leaves only two ways to reduce the dissonance: change your behaviors moving forward or forget your past sins.

Most of the time, people tend toward the latter. Forgetting past sins is a lot easier than turning over a new leaf. So our minds whitewash memories of our unethical acts, meaning that these acts become fuzzier over time compared to other types of memories. And as these tainted memories fade, so do our motives to change our ways for the better.

It's here that rituals of atonement have maximum effect. They don't let us forget; they force us to verbally admit our guilt. For

Catholics, the days between Ash Wednesday and Easter—a period known as Lent—are, like the Jewish Days of Awe, a time for self-reflection and seeking forgiveness. And while Catholics can take part in the sacrament of confession—a ritual for forgiveness—at any time during the year, they're especially encouraged to do so during Lent.

We can all agree that admitting our failings isn't fun. It often makes us feel guilty or ashamed, both of which can discourage us from taking part in the ritual in the first place. So to make admitting sins easier, Catholic confession, like Judaism's viddui, offers some anonymity. Where Jews confess by reciting a list of sins in unison—an act that prevents other people from knowing which sins apply to any given person—Catholics utter their sins in isolation.

Before taking part in confession, Catholics usually settle into a church pew to pray. They keep their eye on a spot along the wall, waiting for a door or thick curtain to open, signaling the confessional chamber is now free. They slip inside the small, dimly lit room and take their place at a kneeler in front of a screen. Soon the priest, who is sitting in a chamber on the other side of the screen, slides open a panel and welcomes the penitent. The dividing screen lets sound pass through but not light, to protect the person's identity. "Bless me, Father for I have sinned . . ." the confessor begins, and over the next few minutes admits transgressions in hushed tones. After a prayer, the priest offers absolution for the sins, and the penitent leaves, usually with instructions for further prayers or acts of penance to improve their soul. As with reciting the viddui, sins are front and center in consciousness, making it feel more pressing to atone for them. Whitewashing becomes much more difficult.

But there's another tool that we can use every day to achieve similar goals: meditation. While, as we've seen, it helps people grapple with life's temporary nature, its primary goal is to end the suffering of all beings. One of the best ways to do this is by helping people develop deep, abiding compassion.

For Buddhists, two intertwined virtues lead to well-being: wisdom and compassion. As we discussed earlier, Buddhists believe that our tendency to assume things have essences—to assign them permanent attributes and categories—is a problematic illusion. Whether or not you agree with this theological principle, it's clear that meditation helps us to see the world more clearly rather than through our habitual and often harmful lenses. In so doing, it helps us to pause and see each other not as white, Black, Democrat, or Republican but as fellow humans worthy of compassion and care. That sense of shared similarity allows our deeper empathy, generosity, and forgiveness—the emotions that underlie connection—to guide our actions.

This notion of a compassion technology may sound a little too good to be true, so let me offer some evidence. A few years back, my research group decided to test whether meditation can make people more compassionate. We recruited people from the Boston area who had never meditated before to take part in an eight-week experiment. Half of them came to campus once a week to learn meditation from a Buddhist lama. Between those trainings, they practiced at home guided by recordings the lama created. We put the other half—the control group—on a waiting list to train with the lama.

At the end of eight weeks, we had people come to the lab one at a time. We told them we'd be giving them memory and attention tests to see if meditating improved these functions. But that wasn't true. We were testing their kindness.

When each person arrived, they entered a waiting room that had three chairs. Two of these chairs were already occupied. So, as

any normal person would do, they sat in the remaining chair. Unbeknownst to them, the occupants of the other chairs were actors
working for us. A few minutes later, the third actor would appear.
She was using crutches, looking pained. She winced every time
she moved her foot, which was encased in one of those medical
boots people use when their foot is broken (which it wasn't). As
she entered the waiting room, the other actors ignored her while
thumbing their phones. With no place to sit, she'd move toward
the wall and lean uncomfortably against it.

The question for us was whether the person in our study—
the only one here who wasn't an actor—would ignore her too or
would ease her pain by offering their chair. To our astonishment,
50 percent of those who had meditated for the past eight weeks
quickly offered her their seat; only 16 percent of the control group
did the same. That's a huge difference in showing compassion. To
be sure this wasn't a fluke, we repeated the experiment and found
similar results.

Finally, we ran a third study, this time looking at forgiveness.
To make a long story short, when people returned to the lab after
meditating or doing different types of brain exercises for a few
weeks, we had them write and deliver a short speech about their
life goals to a partner. The partner was an actor who gave them
pretty negative feedback about their speech—a setup that's been
shown to evoke a desire for revenge. No one likes being told their
life goals don't make sense! Yet, when we gave people an opportunity to inflict some mild physical pain on the partner who insulted them, most of those who had meditated didn't take us up on
the offer. But those who hadn't meditated jumped at the chance to
seek revenge (which, of course, we didn't let happen).

A month or two of meditation certainly doesn't make one an
expert. The full benefits come over years of practice. But when you

combine our findings with others showing short periods of meditation also make people more generous, the evidence is plain that it can quickly make us take up the virtues that bring on both inner peace and stronger connections with other people.

The Meghiya Sutta, a central Buddhist text, explicitly argues that having good friends is as central to well-being as is virtuous conduct and insight into impermanence. Here again is a message echoed by many other religions—a message that science is finally deciphering through its empirical lens. Compassion, service, generosity, forgiveness. While in the short term such feelings and actions seem only to help others, the social networks they form and strengthen ultimately aid the givers themselves. It's *why* giving feels good. It's why friendship heals the body and mind. It's why avoiding these virtues can bring the greatest regrets as our days wind down. It's why our minds turn toward social concerns ever more intently as we age to ensure our relationships with others don't dissolve.

For those entering midlife, I'd recommend starting a meditation practice because it speeds this process of reorientation. Fortunately, many religious traditions offer forms of meditation that can be practiced frequently. And most can be adapted to a secular context.

As for Yom Kippur or Lent, the practices underpinning them can be applied more regularly too. You can set your own times to make amends and do good works—times that ensure years won't go by without you considering seeking forgiveness or working to help others in your family or community. Likewise, you can make it a point, even daily, to reflect on what it would mean if you were to die today. To consider both what you would regret and how, beginning in this moment, you might change to reduce that regret. Whether it's Thomas à Kempis's advice or Laura Carstensen's research tactic—both of which boil down to imagining you'll be dead very soon—the result will be the same: a temporary reorientation of your values and motives. And if you make it a habit, what's temporary can become permanent.

So if and when the angst of midlife arises, the main thing to remember is that you need to address the shattering of two illusions—mortality and individualism—at the same time to get the maximum benefit. As religious leaders realized long ago, the mind is loath to change ideals and strategies if it's been reaping rewards from them. Only after they repeatedly fail to provide happiness due to our changing circumstances and bodies will our minds come to realize that selfish pursuits have become pointless, and only after that will our minds finally change what they value. By then, though, precious time will have been lost—time when we've been suppressing anxiety or a nagging dissatisfaction by clinging to an expired phase of life rather than adapting to a new one. These are problems that the wisdom of religion can help you avoid as your skin begins to wrinkle and your hair turns gray.

Saying Goodbye:
All That Lives Must Die

The question of what, if anything, follows death can frighten anyone approaching it. For those who remain behind, grief can be almost as unnerving. And while the course of that grief can and does vary, the pain it brings is never welcome. When someone we love dies, we hurt. It feels as if there's a wound deep in our chests. In fact, the brain interprets separation from one we love as physical pain. And the longer we grieve, the greater the toll it takes on our minds and bodies.

I'm not saying that grief is bad. It's a natural and necessary part of life. In many ways, it honors the person that has left us. But if it goes on too long, it can prematurely extinguish the joys we have yet to feel in the time *we* have left in this world—something departed souls would not wish for those they leave behind. For these reasons, all the world's religions have practices meant to ease life's final step, both for those who are taking it and for those who are saying goodbye.

Moving Beyond the Veil

When a Catholic is close to death, a priest administers Last Rites. As the plural form indicates, this isn't a single ritual; it actually comprises three distinct ones: confession, anointing of the sick, and Holy Communion. And while each of these rites is familiar to Catholics, as they're not reserved for people approaching death when conducted separately, when slightly modified and packaged together in Last Rites, the combination is exquisitely suited to meet the needs at hand: comforting people during the process of death while also preparing them to enter what they hope to be a heavenly afterlife.

While confession usually takes place in private chambers, in the case of Last Rites, it is done face-to-face. Here, the intimacy and empathy that comes from the priest's face outweighs any concerns about anonymity. People near death don't need to worry about keeping up appearances.

The beauty of confession is that it offers an objective assurance of forgiveness. Unlike praying for God's pardon, which doesn't offer a direct response, when a priest forgives a believer in God's name, they can be sure they're forgiven. And when facing a transition to the afterlife where entering a heavenly domain depends upon possessing a virtuous soul, confession can be quite comforting. It also offers a way for people to admit and thus face failings that they might have been harboring silently for years. It can be nothing short of cathartic; it can relieve long-standing guilt and the psychological pain it causes. In those moments when a priest touches a person near death and says that God understands and loves them, the peace of forgiveness envelops them, and their bodies relax.

The second ritual of Last Rites is the anointing of the sick—a ritual that Catholic doctrine describes as meant to offer strength, peace, and comfort. I described this ritual in chapter 5, as it's also used for healing the seriously ill. But when death seems imminent, the ritual's meaning and symbolism shift. As the priest places holy oil on the dying person's head, he also asks three things of God. First, that God help the person endure the pain and anxiety that may come with death's approach. Second, that God forgive the person of their sins—something that can be important especially if the dying person is too frail or otherwise unable to complete a full confession. And third, that the person be raised up to heaven.

At this point, with the mind calmed and the soul prepared, the only thing remaining is the journey itself. And that brings us to viaticum.

Viaticum, or the final Holy Communion, is the third ritual of Last Rites. Its name pretty much says it all, at least in Latin. It means the provisions you need to bring with you for a journey. Unlike other Christians, Catholics believe that the wafer of bread and sip of wine they consume during Communion are the actual body and blood of Jesus Christ (rather than symbolic representations of his body and blood). In the Bible's Gospel (the Book of John), Jesus specifically teaches that he will abide in whoever eats his flesh and drinks his blood in this form, and will raise them up to eternal life when they die.

Because of this teaching, Catholics who receive Communion near the time of death believe that God is physically and spiritually with them and will bring them to heaven. The ritual's intent is clear, as the priest adds the words "may the Lord Jesus Christ protect you and lead you to eternal life"—words that aren't said as part of the normal Communion ritual—as he offers this final Communion wafer.

Hindu rituals for the dying, though springing from an entirely different theology, serve the same functions. When it becomes clear that a person is near death, Hindu customs dictate that they should be brought home if not there already. Hinduism places a strong emphasis on the belief that the dying should pass in the place that they find most comfortable and secure. Usually that means their own bedroom. The goal for the days or hours the person remains alive is to prepare the soul for its next rebirth. The dying person is laid down with their head facing east toward the next sunrise, and a lamp is usually placed next to them as a symbol of lighting their way.

As death—or "the great departure," as Hindus call it—approaches, the dying person's family surrounds them to sing hymns, offer prayers, and provide company and comfort. But the person themself repeats a mantra to benefit their karma. The Gayatri Mantra is often used:

We meditate on the glory of the Creator;
Who has created the universe;
Who is worthy of worship
Who is the embodiment of knowledge and light;
Who is the remover of all sin and ignorance;
May He enlighten our intellect.

Both the Catholic and Hindu rites focus on the needs of the dying, not the living. And paramount among these needs is reducing uncertainty and anxiety about the most mysterious transition of life. Last Rites, for example, is never given to a corpse. If it's certain that death has come and believed that the person's soul has departed, the time for Last Rites has passed. Likewise in Hinduism. Once death has occurred, the body is immediately prepared for its cremation. It is laid in the entryway of the home on a low cot or on the floor, symbolizing its return to the earth, and covered with a white cloth. The point here is that dead bodies aren't anxious; dying people are.

At any point in life, uncertainty brings anxiety. And the greater the possible threat, the greater the fear. So when it comes to facing the possibility of a complete and permanent end to the self, feeling anxious makes sense. In fact, prominent thinkers from Durkheim to Freud to Kierkegaard have argued that the fear of death is so central to the human condition that it's the primary reason religion emerged. While I don't buy that, as religions provide tools for dealing with many of life's challenges, I certainly agree that death is one of the biggest.

As it does in so many areas, belief is likely to play a helpful role here. Many studies have explored whether belief in God reduces anxiety about death. And the consensus is that it does. By combining the results of a hundred different studies, researchers found an intriguing pattern. In general, as religious faith goes up, unease about death goes down. But there was also a quirk of sorts in this finding. Although it's true that, on average, people who were the least religious worried more about dying compared to those with the strongest faith, there was a slight bump up in the middle of the continuum. People who had some religious beliefs but also harbored doubts were the most anxious of all. In other words, strong believers are less anxious about death than committed atheists are, but the people who aren't sure what they believe about God are the most anxious of all.

If you stop to think about it, this pattern makes good sense. For all but the most steadfast atheists, death represents a transition to another domain. For some, that transition is a certainty; for others, it's a possibility. But either way, a threshold looms large. And that means rites for the dying are, in essence, another rite of passage. In fact, they might seem the most important rite of passage. They don't help you become an adult or get married; they help determine your eternity. Part of the increased anxiety among those unsure about God surely stems from uncertainty about what, if anything, is on the other side of that threshold. But part also likely comes from a concern about worth: being a weak believer usually means not following a faith's, and by extension God's, rules as assiduously.

We've seen that, unlike other rituals, completing rites of passage requires more than just managing stress and unease; there's also something to prove. When you move from child to adult, you need to prove your competence. When you move from living in this world to entering the next, you need to prove your worth—not to the community, but to God or to the scales of karma. If they're to ease the transition, rituals surrounding death must lessen the anxiety about whether you've met the requirements to go someplace better.

In Last Rites, confession and the anointing of the sick serve this purpose. Both are designed to cleanse the soul of sin and let a dying person believe that God will view them as worthy. In Hindu rites, the recitation of mantras serves the same goal. It adds points of virtue to a soul that, for most believers, is about to be reborn. But on a deeper neuropsychological level, theses rites provide another type of comfort. One for the anxieties related not to the future but to the moment at hand: the body's experience of looming death.

The touch and handholding of a priest, the slowed and rhythmic breathing that goes with reciting mantras or the rosary (which, though not formally part of Last Rites, is often done by Catholics as death draws near), the felt connection with God that comes from viaticum, all work to calm the body and mind as signals run up and down the vagus nerve. The goal, again, is to reduce the fight-or-flight response that often accompanies anxiety and allow people to feel safer and more peaceful as death overtakes them.

That quirk in the relation between belief and anxiety—the one showing people with ambivalent beliefs about God were the most anxious—might seem to suggest that there's a small benefit to being an atheist when approaching death. Atheists weren't as calm as strong believers, but they were a bit less anxious than those who weren't sure about there being an afterlife. This seems logical, since the absence of God also entails an absence of any kind of afterlife. If nothing follows death, an atheist might have little reason to worry whether they've prepared themselves properly. But then I recall the old saying: "There are no atheists in foxholes." As a scientist, I'm not persuaded by aphorisms, but I also recognize that aphorisms might contain truth. And from what we can tell, this is the case with facing death. It can make people find belief.

While we can't ethically conduct certain types of research with people as they rapidly approach death, we can ask people to think about death at other times. And when they do, even atheists show an uptick in suspecting God might exist. It's not that they'll suddenly say they believe in God, but they do become less certain in their denials.

For believers (and for reformed atheists), the afterlife generally falls into one of two types. In many Western religions, the next world is similar to this one: people keep their identities and memories intact as they enter a (hopefully) heavenly realm to be reunited with loved ones. In Eastern religions, it's a bit more complex. First, there's the issue of reincarnation, which usually means that death precedes a new life. Hinduism and Buddhism also teach that after a soul reaches a pinnacle of wisdom or enlightenment, it can break free from the cycle of rebirth and move into a better state.

Beliefs vary widely on the nature of this better state. Some

Buddhists believe that those ready to break free from rebirth merge into a kind of emptiness or universal force. Others say they first enter a paradisical realm known as the Pure Land. Where some see the individual's mind being extinguished, others see a person choosing to become an angel-like bodhisattva—a being that devotes itself to reducing the suffering of all other sentient creatures.

Of course, I don't know what happens after death or which, if any, religions have it right. But the idea that our consciousness lives on makes death feel less like an extinction and more like a transition. And religions excel at helping people make transitions. Believing in a divine being or force who created what's on the other side of the ultimate threshold makes the transition easier.

In psychological terms, I see no reason to fight such beliefs. None of us know whether there's an afterlife. But we do know that the prospect of one would bring some peace of mind for believers. So why not believe? In some ways, you might be unnecessarily torturing yourself if you don't. The only reason to avoid a belief in the afterlife would be if holding one caused some harm in the here and now. Though some prominent atheists have argued that such is the case, the data doesn't support this argument.

Steven Pinker summed up this position succinctly when he said that "belief in an afterlife is a malignant delusion which devalues actual lives and discourages action that would make them longer, safer, and happier." He made this statement in response to many Evangelicals' demands to end lockdowns during the COVID-19 epidemic. He contended that people of faith would be more willing to take risks with their lives on earth because they assumed their deaths would only mean a quicker transition to paradise.

I doubt that Evangelicals' opposition to social distancing had much to do with their belief in heaven. It's much more likely that political ideology was the driving factor. Still, the notion that belief in heaven leads people to devalue life on earth pervades atheist messaging. And while there are notorious cases of deadly behaviors enabled by a quest for the afterlife, mostly among apocalyptic cults, those cases are extremely isolated and rare. In general, there's no evidence that belief in life after death poses any problem for the believer or for others.

One finding that's often used to support the atheists' argument is a study from 2015 suggesting that simple reminders of God lead people to say they'll take more risks in life. While this study garnered a lot of attention when it was first reported, its results didn't hold up upon further examination. Subsequent studies with more people failed to show any link between thinking about God and increased risk-taking. What's more, if you look at people's actual behaviors, increased religiosity, which usually goes along with increased beliefs in an afterlife, is clearly linked to better health and longer life, as we saw in chapter 5. Believers smoke less, drink less, avoid risky sex, and use seat belts more. In fact, some religions explicitly instruct followers to keep themselves healthy. Judaism in particular tells believers to avoid physical dangers and anything that could pose major harm to health.

So while none of us can say with certainty what will happen when we close our eyes for the final time, neither can we say that expecting something will take place—that we will move on in some form—is a harmful delusion. If anything, the belief itself seems helpful, both as we live our lives and face their ends.

Whatever your faith, or absence thereof, there's another lesson to take from rituals surrounding death: providing comfort through opportunities for forgiveness can ease people's minds. We've all heard of deathbed confessions. And most of those aren't made to priests. Giving people one last opportunity to seek forgiveness for the sins they've carried with them is an act of mercy. And relieving a dying person's guilt can bring them immense relief. For that reason, I suggest offering your friends and loved ones opportunities for forgiveness. Offer space and even gently encourage them to open up about regrets or transgressions that they might have been harboring for years. And do so as a priest would: Listen, don't judge, work to heal rather than to condemn. In the fleeting time they have left, you might be surprised at how readily the dying might grasp an opportunity to discuss issues that they had steadfastly refused to earlier in life.

Religious practices show us another, more physical way to comfort those who will leave us soon. As in Hindu tradition, I'd recommend placing a person in familiar environs if at all possible. I'd also suggest using contemplative techniques. If a person isn't religious, mantras, rosaries, and the like won't have much influence upon them. But other strategies that produce similar bodily changes can help. Breathe deeply together. Sing or hum favorite tunes together. Spend a few minutes focusing their and your attention on objects of beauty. Hold hands. In so doing, you'll raise their vagal tone. And via synchronous movement, you'll help them subconsciously feel less isolated in their last days and hours in this world.

When they pass, though, it's time to comfort ourselves—the ones who remain in this world. And the quicker that good work begins, the better.

Grief Nudges

For Jews, the period of bereavement is divided into three principal parts: *aninut*, shiva, and *sheloshim. Aninut*, which means "deep sorrow," begins at the moment of a person's death and lasts until their burial. It's typically a brief period, lasting hours to a day or two, but it's emotionally intense. During this time, the people closest to the deceased—spouses, children, parents, and siblings—take on a religious status known as *onein*. The Hebrew root of this word means to be under pressure, and given the shock they're likely feeling, as well as the need to make preparations for burial quickly, the label makes good sense. As a marker of the pain they're feeling, these close family members would traditionally place a tear over their heart in clothing they will wear throughout the mourning period of shiva. Today, though, many opt to pin a torn black ribbon to their clothing to symbolize the same. This marker of mourning, or *kriah*, is one that other Jews recognize as an indication to approach them appropriately.

In many ways, the period of *aninut* isn't that different from what happens in other religions, except for being somewhat more formalized. In all religions the time from death to burial is one when the family is given space and support to grieve as they make the necessary arrangements. From a psychological perspective, though, perhaps the most important aspect of *aninut* is its brevity. As Rabbi Benjamin Resnick, a scholar of Jewish mysticism and the head rabbi for one of Chicago's largest Jewish day schools, points out, "As Jews, we bury the dead quickly, not only as a kindness to them but as a reminder to us. Life can and must continue in the wake of even the most tragic losses."

Accordingly, at the end of the funeral, family members' status changes from *onein* to *avelin*. From being "under pressure" to being full-fledged mourners. Now shiva commences, and with it the full attention of extended family, friends, and community members turns to healing the bereaved.

"Shiva" comes from the Hebrew word meaning seven, as it usually lasts seven days. Following the funeral, it's customary for everyone to return to the mourning family's home for a meal and condolences, with the food often provided by neighbors or friends.

In fact, the act of providing food or other support to a grieving family is considered a "mitzvah," or "commandment," from God. It's not just something nice to do; it's something you have to do.

The mourners prepare their home for shiva by covering mirrors and lighting a candle in remembrance of the deceased. Over the coming days, they're not to worry about shaving, styling their hair, laundering their clothes, or putting on their best outfits for visitors. They'll also sit low to the ground, either on specially made stools or on pillows, while guests arrive. Traditionally, they also leave the doors to their homes unlocked so that family and friends can enter easily to pay their respects.

As each of the seven days of shiva unfolds, friends, extended family, and community members continue to visit. By custom, guests continue the mitzvah of bringing food for the family. When they arrive at the home, they don't rush up to the mourners to express condolences but rather wait for them to begin a conversation. They follow the mourner's lead. If they want to talk about their loss, that's where the conversation goes. If they want to distract themselves by talking about sports, that's fine too. The point is to give them what they need at the moment. But at some point during shiva, conversations among guests and mourners invariably turn to reminiscing about the deceased.

Shiva customs also require formal prayer services in the mourners' home, which usually take place three times a day. But for these services to occur, religious law dictates that a minyan—at least ten Jewish adults—be present. As part of the ritual, the shiva minyan recites several prayers together, with the mourner's kaddish being a primary one.

While the funeral and mourning rituals of all religions can help with grief, there's a particular brilliance in shiva. From a psychological standpoint, all its elements, down to covering mirrors and crouching on low stools, help a grieving mind. To see why is to understand how people move through grief. But before we do that, I want to dispel a common notion concerning grief's stages.

If you were to ask most people, or even Dr. Google, about the grieving process, you'd get the same answer. Grief has five stages: denial, anger, bargaining, depression, and finally acceptance. But if you look at the actual research, there's no evidence for this at all. In saying this, I don't mean that these stages never occur or won't apply to some people, but they don't reflect the norm. And if you think about, it makes sense. It's very unlikely that a middle-aged person would feel the same way about the death of their ninety-year-old mother after a painful illness as they would about the un-anticipated and tragic death of their teenage son in a car accident.

This doesn't mean the grieving process is random, though. There's a good deal of research showing that it follows certain patterns. The specific nature of these patterns depends on how much grief people feel and for how long they feel it. The psychologist George Bonanno, one of the world's leading experts on bereavement and resilience, finds that about 92 percent of people follow one of three trajectories. The largest category is what he terms *resilient*. While these people certainly feel grief when a loved one dies, it's manageable. Yes, they're in pain, but depression doesn't spike. They can carry on with the daily responsibilities of life. About 67 percent of people follow this trajectory. Another 15 percent of people experience grief in a more debilitating way—one that hinders their ability to work, to take good care of themselves, and even to find any joy in life for extended periods of time. This pattern—what Bonanno calls common grief—is characterized by a significant rise in depression that can take up to eighteen months to fade. And yet another 10 percent—those following the chronic grief trajectory—become permanently depressed.

Overall, Bonanno's research shows that most people do overcome the grief and depression that surround loss. But even among that majority, there exist important differences not only in the intensity of the distress they suffer but also how quickly they move through it. The trick with grief then, isn't to avoid it completely but to shape its intensity and time frame. While dealing with a loss doesn't always lead to depression and debilitating emotional pain, that's only true if it's not too chronic or intense. If distress and depression go on too long, they can often lead people to act in ways that make the long-term situation even worse: using addictive drugs to dull the pain or socially isolating themselves, which will ultimately intensify it.

So the goal of spiritual technologies isn't to prevent grief—some grief is natural and necessary—but rather to nudge it along. To put people on Bonanno's resilience trajectory where they'll feel grief but avoid intense, long-term, harmful anguish.

Demonstrating the power of religion to help, research shows that taking part in religious activities supports the bereaved, especially by reducing the duration of their grief. Three main factors play a role here, as they principally determine how people move through grief. And while the rituals of all religions leverage one or two of them, shiva uses all three.

The first is the one that's most pervasive: eulogizing. Anyone who has ever been to a funeral or mourning ritual knows that everyone there spends a good deal of time reminiscing about the deceased. Common as this practice is, it might seem counterintuitive at first. If you just lost a job you loved or an award for which you were being considered, you probably wouldn't want to spend much time dwelling on it. You lost it; it's gone. It hurts. Best to move on.

When it comes to people we've lost, the opposite holds true. Reinforcing their memories, especially in an idealized form, keeps them with us. In a way, it prevents us from losing them twice—once when they die and again if their memory fades. In fact, Bonanno has found a clear link between positive memories of lost loved ones and healthy grief trajectories. Those who are resilient retain solid memories. Those in common grief have clouded memories until their depression lifts, and those in chronic grief have difficulty recalling positive memories at all. So reinforcing positive memories moves people toward resilience. And where almost all religious mourning rituals do this as part of a funeral—or, in the case of Christian wakes, for a day or two before the funeral—shiva ensures it goes on for a longer period following the funeral—the precise time when grief trajectories are beginning to unfold, and thus are most easily changed.

The second factor centers on acceptance. Coming to see the passing of loved ones as a sad but natural part of life reduces feelings of anger and cosmic persecution that some might otherwise feel. It's true that you don't need religion to view death as natural. Even young people will sometimes die unexpectedly in accordance with the laws of probability. A usually safe vaccine or medical procedure will on rare occasions kill a few. Car accidents can happen to anyone. We all accept these facts in the abstract, but when someone we love is the statistic, logic offers no comfort.

Here religion offers another benefit. Some people turn to the idea that God works in mysterious ways, or that we're here only until God calls our number. The sense that life isn't random, that there's a reason why a loved one has moved on, can sometimes help people accept a death more readily. Shiva offers an added nudge toward acceptance when mourners recite the kaddish together. As Rabbi Lord Jonathan Sacks noted, "'Kaddish' is a prayer we say when we mourn, but oddly enough, it's to do with life rather than death. And that is a way of bringing us comfort when we most feel a sense of loss. We reconnect with life." By proclaiming God's glory and asking for peace and blessings on earth, kaddish reinforces that God isn't to be doubted or blamed for a death. Death is natural, and God wants His people to go on living in peace and happiness.

The third and most effective factor in reducing the intensity and duration of grief is instrumental support. This term refers to a very specific type of help: showing up. A person can have lots of Facebook friends or Twitter followers, but most of these people won't drop everything to offer in-person aid and comfort when it's needed. In times of loss and grief, the benefits that come from having people spend time with you, cook for you, shop for you cannot be overstated.

In this regard, shiva shines. By making it a mitzvah—a sacred obligation of the faith—to help and support mourners, shiva ensures that they will have frequent access to instrumental support and company. Of course, Judaism isn't the only religion where people visit mourners and bring food. But it is one of the few that ritualizes instrumental support in this way. People *will* show up for seven days to provide help, company, and a minyan to pray. They have to. And that rule can make all the difference for how the mourners move through their grief.

Shiva has even more psychological nudges baked into it. At first blush, covering mirrors and forsaking grooming wouldn't seem to have any obvious links to mourning. But both serve a psychological function: reducing people's focus on themselves. When you look into a mirror, your attention necessarily centers on yourself—a fact that both logic and research makes clear. When you're trying to adjust your hair, remove some of it by shaving, or pick out your best clothing, you're again thinking about what makes *you* look good. And many psychological studies have found that self-focus intensifies whatever emotion a person is feeling.

Speaking directly to the shiva customs, researchers have demonstrated that looking into a mirror when we're sad makes that sadness worse. Other experiments have found that when thoughts about ourselves increase, they can amplify and perpetuate negative feelings. So when Jews cover their mirrors and ignore their own appearances, they're using psychological tools proven to reduce distress.

Judaism isn't the only religion that strives to minimize self-focus during mourning. Certain sects of Hinduism cover mirrors in the home following a death. You'll also find it at Irish wakes. None of these traditions do so because they have data showing it reduces grief. They each have their own rationales based on beliefs about respecting the dead, hiding gateways to the spiritual realm, etc. But it's likely that these customs persist because, over time, they've helped the grieving feel a bit less distraught.

Shiva also encourages mourners to sit low to the ground. Theologically, this custom is often traced to a passage from the Book of Job that describes how Job's friends sat with him low to the ground for seven days in his grief. Symbolically, this type of sitting is also believed to reflect that people feel "low" when they mourn. While both of these are true, sitting low serves another purpose at a neurological level. When you sit lower than you would on a normal chair or stool, it's physically uncomfortable. In trying to place your feet flat on the ground, your knees will be high, meaning that your thighs will be at a less than 90-degree angle to your shins and you'll slouch forward. If you try to straighten your legs, you'll be in an even more unnatural position.

Sitting on the floor for an extended period, as some do during shiva, is equally uncomfortable, as it requires a good deal of core strength to keep your torso upright without anything to lean against. Any ergonomics expert will tell you that either of these positions will place a painful strain on your lower back. Getting up will ease the pain. And if you follow this sequence every so often—as mourners are likely to do while sitting shiva—it means you'll repeatedly experience mild pain followed by relief of that pain.

Research shows that repeated offsets of mild pain increase feelings of well-being and reduce grief and rumination. And given that grief and rumination often run on a continuous loop during bereavement, repeating the process of sitting low and rising to stand can help reduce the psychological pain mourners feel.

Finally, there's the minyan itself. Communal prayer, which often involves some synchronous swaying, strengthens psychological bonds during shiva. Remember, synchronous movement also makes people feel more compassionate toward one another—a feeling that can offer a huge benefit when some of them are grieving.

All told, the period of shiva offers a protective cocoon of sorts in which mourners can adjust to the loss of someone they love. But as the seventh day approaches (the sixth after the day of the funeral), the time draws near to gradually reenter normal life. Two concepts here are operative: *gradual* and *reentry*. The idea of reentry is important, as it implies that the mourners are resilient—that they can and should begin to move on from mourning. This is why, at the end of shiva, the mourners rise from their low seats and, supported by family and friends, leave their home for a walk around the neighborhood. This first trip outdoors serves as a marker both to the community and the mourners themselves that they've entered a new phase.

This brings us to the second operative concept: *gradual*. It would be unreasonable and unkind to assume that at the end of seven days, people's grief would be gone and life would again feel completely normal. So the end of shiva doesn't mark the end of mourning but rather the *beginning* of the end of mourning. The outdoor walk begins the third period of Jewish grieving, *sheloshim*.

The word *sheloshim* means thirty in Hebrew, and that's how many days it lasts. During *sheloshim*, the bereaved slowly return to the normal rhythms of life. People begin to adjust their ways of interacting with the bereaved. But there are restrictions too. For example, mourners typically refrain from attending celebratory social events without the hosts feeling insulted. This, too, is a kindness, as it would be difficult for them to be appropriately joyous so close to losing a loved one. The end of *sheloshim* is usually marked by a memorial service in honor of the deceased. It's another opportunity to reinforce positive memories of them.

As I noted above, all these ritualistic tools aren't solely the province of Judaism. Many religions share some elements with shiva. For example, in addition to covering mirrors, some Hindu traditions also incorporate several memorial meals during which families often serve foods that were the favorites of the deceased, and the guests say prayers and share good memories of them. The rituals of Islam require Muslims to observe a three-day period of mourning, during which the bereaved are relieved of most responsibilities and remain at home to receive instrumental support from extended family and friends.

For all their psychological power, these ritualistic techniques still fall short of one goal: keeping the relationship with a loved one going. Whether that's objectively even possible, of course, depends on your faith. But to see how it can work, let's look to a religious tradition that incorporates veneration of dead. The Chinese burn fake currency, called ghost money or joss paper, to benefit their dead relatives. Though its source is unclear, the ritual seems to have originated in a Taoist belief that the dead can and will use this money to purchase what they desire in the afterlife. The more money burned, the more they have to spend on luxuries.

According to Chinese beliefs, ancestors also have the power to influence what happens in the present. And so by honoring them, people are also seeking their aid and assistance. In some ways, it continues the relationship people had with their elders when they were still alive. In fact, the gift giving can get quite elaborate. In Chinese communities there are often shops that sell hundreds of objects constructed from joss paper. People burn paper replicas of houses, clothing, gadgets—you name it—for their ancestors to use as the smoke brings these gifts to the heavenly realm.

I love this ritual because it provides a way to keep expressing gratitude to people who have passed. And not just with money, but by actually spending time thinking about what they might like or need. Doing this serves two psychological purposes. The first has to do with joy. The mind interprets giving as pleasure—giving to anyone, but especially when it's to someone about whom we truly care. And when this giving occurs near the time of death, as it would at a funeral, that spark of joy can help slightly to ease despair.

People also burn gifts on their ancestors' birthdays and the anniversaries of their deaths. This means they have a continual way for interacting with those who are now gone. This second psychological purpose—the feeling of ongoing connection—also helps combat lingering grief: the relationship continues, albeit in a different form. By embracing this belief, people come to accept the notion that death isn't the end but, rather, a transition. And one that, when their own time comes to move beyond the veil, will help reunite them with those who have already passed while also allowing them to keep some contact with those they'll leave behind in this world.

In dealing with your own or others' grief, you can adapt many of the tools these mourning rituals use. No matter your faith or lack thereof, you probably already use eulogizing to some extent to reinforce positive memories of the deceased. Setting times to do it more regularly, not just during the funeral proper or days surrounding it but over the following weeks or months, can magnify its benefit.

Finding a way to ensure instrumental support for the bereaved is also paramount. Outside of a few religious rituals, like those of shiva, there are few set guidelines to make sure people show up whenever they're needed. I was raised Christian, and while it's certainly seen as noble to offer comfort and help to the bereaved following a funeral, it's not ritually formalized in any way. If that's true in your group of family or friends, one way to fill that gap is to start doing it yourself. Set a norm that others can copy. Or better yet, create your own secular shiva. What truly matters isn't the exact texts of the prayers, but the togetherness, the sensitivity, and the actions inherent in the ritual. Eat together. Schedule times to gather for the first few weeks. Recall fond memories of the deceased together. Sing songs, maybe even the favorites of the person who has passed.

And don't forget those grief nudges. Cover your mirrors. Forget about ironing your best clothes for visitors; you don't need to be the host or hostess. Also, do something that provides a bit of physical discomfort and then relive it a few times a day. Maybe something that's even good for you, like exercise. I realize that in the throes of grief, finding the motivation to work out can be difficult. But that's why ritualizing it can be helpful.

When you're grieving, you might also consider giving. You don't have to believe in the duties of ancestor worship for it to help. You don't even need to believe in an afterlife. Remember, just as the brain interprets loss as pain, it interprets giving as pleasure, no matter whom you give to. So rather than burn an offering to honor a passed soul if doing so doesn't have meaning for you, give to someone else in that person's name. Even better, spend some time thinking about what the person you lost valued in life. What they stood for. With that in mind, thoughtfully choose whom or what to help—a person or entity whose aid would bring your loved one joy and satisfaction. That too can be a kind of joss paper.

Perhaps most important of all, strive to stay attuned to the changing needs of mourners. If you're not Jewish, you don't need to strictly follow the timeline of shiva and *sheloshim*. But you do need to meet mourners where they are. A good way to do that might be by adapting an idea the Victorians used over a century ago. They used the color of clothing to mark stages of grief. Close to the time of a loved one's death, they'd wear black clothing as a symbol of the pain. But as time passed and grief began to lighten, so too did the color of clothing: from gray and lilac during half mourning to lights and white at the end. The colors signaled where the bereaved were in their stages of sorrow—information that allowed others to approach them more appropriately.

When we do emerge from grief's shadow, there's no denying that life will be different. It's not only our relationships that will have changed; we will have too. Christianity often speaks of the power of suffering to help people become closer to God. Whereas Buddhists understand suffering as the normal condition of life and use meditation as a way overcome it, Christians see suffering as a way to imitate Jesus, and thus become more Christlike. For them, accepting suffering is a way to banish any sense of pride, hubris, or entitlement. If God in the human form of Jesus could accept suffering, so could they. So while suffering wasn't a goal in and of itself, it did offer a way to cleanse the soul through acceptance and, similar to meditation, help make people more compassionate and loving—a change that would also help their well-being.

While I've said many times that I don't want to debate theology, there is some truth to the notion that suffering well, whether due to grief or other causes, can lead to growth. Work I've done with my colleague Daniel Lim shows time and again that a majority of those who have suffered loss and related adversities in life became more compassionate and altruistic afterward. They have more empathy for other people in distress and are more willing to lend a helping hand in terms of time, money, or effort. They're even more resistant to compassion fatigue—the phenomenon whereby we tend to turn away from growing numbers of people in pain because we feel overwhelmed by the suffering or believe we can't make a difference.

But what does it mean to suffer well? From our work, suffering well means trying to cope positively with it. Don't blame God or fate for tragedies that befall you. Don't adopt the view that life has to be terrible in this world and that every person should therefore only look out for themself. Don't embrace anger or envy. Choosing these responses to adversity limits compassion, and along with it your ability to form relationships that can help sustain you. When tragedy strikes, the people who develop and show empathy and compassion for one another survive it best and go on to better psychological health. In fact, as our work shows, those changes from suffering well are enduring ones. People who accepted suffering without lashing out with blame or anger, who came to understand that even small acts of kindness could lead to change, were the ones who developed an abiding capacity for compassion that helped them build and reinforce meaningful relationships as their lives progressed.

In this way, I believe Christians have a point in saying that suffering can serve a greater purpose. It can make you kinder and strengthen your bonds with others—bonds that can help during times of grief or other troubles. This doesn't mean, of course, that you should look for ways to suffer. Rather, it means that when suffering does come, as it invariably will for each of us when we lose someone we love, we should accept it. Sit with it. Don't rage against it. Recognize the ways it unites you with others; grief and loss are common to us all, irrespective of race, religion, or degree of wealth. Notice how meaningful even the seemingly small kindnesses others show you can be.

The wisdom that comes from this type of suffering, as opposed to the anger and hopelessness that come from different ways of approaching it, can make a big difference in how grief changes us. If we suffer well, it does make us more caring, and that, whatever your faith in God, is a beacon of hope. Yes, death and loss will touch us all. But much as death breeds grief, grief can breed love.

Epilogue

"God is dead. . . . And we have killed him." For Friedrich Nietzsche, who scribbled these words in 1882, this was the Enlightenment's logical result. Reason and empirical observation provided no evidence for God, so we must conclude that It didn't exist. And if God didn't exist, it followed that the moral beliefs and trappings associated with God could be disregarded, as they were based on an illusion of a divine presence in the universe.

Whether Nietzsche's prediction of a moral vacuum was a good thing or a bad one depended on your point of view. Without fear of an omniscient and moralistic God, many people believed humanity would run amok. Greed, selfishness, and violence would rule. For others, like the atheistic Nietzsche himself, it portended a more positive possibility—a freedom of sorts. With no basis to support the old rules of morality, new opportunities would arise for the *Übermensch*— the new and enlightened man—to chart his own path by his own rules and, perhaps, enshrine those rules for others to follow.

Looking back on nearly a century and a half since Nietzsche

wrote these words, I think it's fair to say that neither view was correct. Religion isn't fully dead, though it does appear to be on the decline in its institutional form. As scientific knowledge continues to grow, many have drifted from religion's sway—an exodus that is picking up speed. In the period from 2010 to 2019 alone, the percentage of Americans who identified as Protestants—the most prevalent religious category in the US—dropped from 51 percent to 43 percent. And in that time, the percentage of adults who don't identify with *any* religion rose from 17 percent to 26 percent. Even so, greed and violence haven't overtaken us. Yes, they're still there, but the world's morality hasn't completely crumbled.

The idea of the *Übermensch* hasn't fared much better. In its strongest form, it's illiberal. Who gets to be special and set the agenda? Billionaires? Scientists? Celebrities? Nietzsche wasn't suggesting that a democratic election be held. But even if we soften the idea of *Übermensch* a bit to reflect a person who is living to their fullest potential based on a drive for individual achievement, it doesn't truly offer a route to a fulfilling life. Humans function best when ensconced in caring social relationships, and maintaining such relationships often requires making some sacrifices to individual achievement: taking time off to raise a family or care for an elder, staying close to loved ones rather than moving across the country for a higher salary, devoting time to a volunteer organization in your community rather than putting all your energies toward advancing your career or status.

As Alison Gopnik noted in her review of Steven Pinker's impressive book *Enlightenment Now*, "[Human] values are rooted in emotion and experience as well as reason, in the local as well as the universal.... Family and work, solidarity and autonomy, tradition and innovation are really valuable, and really in tension, in both the lives of individuals and the life of a nation." She goes on to

argue that Western society's view of success—one that regularly places less weight on more traditional, local, and social values—is likely one reason why, even though Pinker argues that the state of the world as a whole is better now than in the past, many people don't feel the joy and satisfaction you'd expect. Striving to satisfy your own desires for status or wealth while neglecting ties to others can often make you feel alienated and lonely. In its best form, religion works to combat that problem by building community.

The trick to a life well lived, then, becomes finding the right balance between focusing on our own needs and those of others. In truth, these two aren't entirely separate, although they often seem to be. Once we consider the element of time, they merge a bit. In the moment, diverting some personal time, money, or effort away from career or personal pursuits to help others can feel like a sacrifice. But in the long run, research shows the ways others will pay those favors back usually outweigh any momentary loss we might feel. Humans are cooperative and social by nature. We do best when we work together, even though doing so can be difficult at times. That's why many of the world's religious rituals work to reinforce our empathy and concern for one another.

I'll admit that humans don't need religion in order to be moral, successful, or happy. The capacity for goodness is literally woven into our DNA. But so, too, is the potential for selfishness and evil. The practice of religion, as opposed to its theological underpinnings, offers an impressive, time-tested array of psychological technologies that augment our biology—to help us solve problems that biological adaptation alone hasn't. And as the nature of those problems changes through time, so do rituals and even religions themselves.

Sometimes, though, the rate of societal change can outpace the ability of formal religions to make necessary modifications. Or the rapid growth of scientific understanding can cast doubt on so many tenets of a faith that its helpful practices get left by the wayside as people abandon it. Now is one of those times. As the statistics above attest, we're moving away from formal religion. At the same time, we've also become less happy, less connected, and thus less satisfied with our lives. Forsaking religious practices surely isn't the only reason for these problems. But in abandoning these practices, we're abandoning tools that can improve our lives every day.

I think people realize this fact. Perhaps not consciously, but we can see it in their yearnings. Findings from the Pew Research Center show that while the number of people who identify as religious has been declining over the past decade, the number of people who identify as spiritual is going up. For example, 27 percent of US adults said they were spiritual but not religious in 2017. That's an 8 percent uptick since Pew last asked this question in 2012. Perhaps most interesting, a closer look at the findings suggests that atheists aren't becoming more spiritual. Rather, those who were religious are turning to different ways of being so: finding a new spirituality while leaving behind more organized religions that no longer seem to resonate.

The question for us going forward, then, centers on how to satisfy the yearning for spiritual tools that have traditionally enriched our lives. People are looking now, as they always have, to religion as a source of support, but not finding exactly what they need. Even today, two-thirds of people who attend church regularly note they do so to give their children a moral foundation, to become better people themselves, or to receive comfort during times of distress and sorrow. But as many turn away from organized religions—sometimes with good reason, depending on the failings of the institution in question—they're losing tools meant to ease their way through life. And even for those who wish to remain associated with a traditional faith, the tools those faiths offer might benefit from some tweaks.

Fortunately, there is a solution. In fact, there are three paths we can take.

Three Paths

No one path is the best to follow because different people have different spiritual needs. For some, the best way to find helpful spiritual tools is by deepening their engagement with traditional faiths. For others, it's loosening the connection to a theology built around a deity while keeping the other aspects of their religion intact. And for a final group, it entails creating something entirely new. All of these approaches are valid. It's not my place to push people toward one option or the other. But what I can offer—where I see the insights of this book playing a role—is in providing constructive advice for how to approach each of these paths if you're so inclined. So let me begin with the first.

One reason people often cite for leaving a faith is that it no longer speaks to them. Some of this sentiment can come from disagreements with the social policies, attitudes, or actions favored by a given religion. But it can also come from another source: the modernization of the day-to-day rituals that surround life and worship. In their attempts to reach out to more people, or to adapt to modernity, aspects of rituals have changed, as has the architecture of sacred spaces.

Take Catholicism as one example. After the Second Vatican Council, many aspects of the Mass changed. Most notably, services were no longer held in Latin but in the congregation's native language. Priests now faced the faithful for the entire service; before Vatican II, they often faced away from their flock. The music at many Masses became folksier. Many churches were built with a more modern aesthetic. While such changes brought Catholic ritual up-to-date, the abandonment of practices that had been honed over centuries reduced some of their psychological power. With less chanting, less incense, and less separation between the pulpit and parishioners, many Catholics felt that the Mass's "magic" had disappeared.

Now, it's important to recognize that this dissatisfaction with modernization doesn't solely come from the old folks missing what they'd grown accustomed to. Many young adults who are interested in the major world faiths actually want them to be more traditional. Consider this: a higher percentage of Jews in their twenties and thirties classify themselves as Orthodox than do those fifty and over. It's true that many of these young people were likely raised Orthodox, as Orthodox families typically have more children than do Reform or Conservative families, but many are also converts, or *baalei teshuva*—those who "return" to God. In a similar vein, fewer Orthodox Jews leave their faith for other denominations compared to Conservative or Reform Jews.

The story among Christians is similar, with mainline denominations continuing to lose numbers at the expense of other, more orthodox faiths. Even the number of young women in the United States deciding to dedicate their lives to God by becoming nuns is rising for the first time in fifty years. Many of the reasons people cite for this interest in the old ways have to do with the beauty of the ceremonies, the structure they give to daily life, and their simultaneous appeal to many of our senses (sight, sound, smell). In fact, surveys of millennials confirm that even in choosing places of worship, they prefer ones with traditional architecture and quiet ambience.

This suggests to me that for those who feel an affinity toward a traditional faith, the best path may be one of return. By that, I don't necessarily mean a return to more sex-segregated policies, reactionary beliefs, or the like, but a return to older rituals and practices that have been honed to leverage the mind through emotion, perceptual cues, and communal activity. The actions, music, and symbols can be the same, even if the theology is updated. These tools speak to our minds in ways that words and beliefs alone do not.

For another group of people, the whole notion of a specific deity, or any deity at all, can seem restrictive or passé. Yet, for these same people, following a set of principles and belonging to a community that shares them—the day-to-day basis of living a religion—remains attractive. Examples of this type can be found in Unitarian Universalism and Humanistic Judaism. Both believe in the value of certain positive moral traits and actions. And both make good use of rituals and practices. They do differ a bit with respect to notions of God. Whereas the Unitarian Universalists welcome all conceptions, including the absence of one, Humanistic Judaism is completely secular. It considers the usual rituals of Judaism not as commands from on high, but as mechanisms with which to bind a community, mark mileposts in life, and celebrate a shared heritage.

To me, religions or movements like these make up a viable second path—the path of refocus. They offer a way to reconsider how you conceive of God, or even whether you believe in It at all, while still taking part in rituals and practices that have proven themselves effective over millennia: birth and death rituals, commitment ceremonies, and other rites of passage. Sometimes the rituals are fixed, as in Humanistic Judaism. Other times they're mixed and matched from different faiths, as in Unitarian Universalism. And still other times, as with the increasingly popular "technology shabbat" (a day away from screen time that's meant to foster reflection and connection with others), they are applied outside the context of any religious beliefs at all. But in each case the rituals are informed by ancient tradition, if not theology.

Finally, there's the path of reformulation. It allows for ultimate flexibility. You don't need to borrow or repurpose rituals. You can create your own. This path isn't as radical as it might appear. Every religion that now exists started somewhere. Every split in certain faiths happened because someone thought there was a newer, better way. Religion has never been static. This time—our time—is no different.

New faiths are being built around AI, for example. In 2015, Anthony Levandowski, a Silicon Valley engineer who co-founded Google's self-driving car program, created a church he called the Way of the Future (WOTF). Although he recently shut it down in the face of several legal battles he was fighting in connection to his work with autonomous vehicles, his vision for AI-based religions is likely a harbinger of things to come. He described WOTF as centered on worshipping a "Godhead based on artificial intelligence." The main idea was to create a "divine" AI with enough power to collect and analyze almost infinite bits of information via the internet about the consequences of people's actions. That knowledge would enable the AI deity to offer guidance on how to live and behave. Levandowski believes that, at some point, an AI will assume control of society, and so he thought it best to shape the nature of that AI so that it'll be beneficent. And to get people to accept this new "deity" and follow its guidance, as well as influence it once it begins to evolve on its own, he thinks new rituals of worship will be needed.

This possibility isn't as far-fetched as it might seem. At the four-hundred-year-old Kodaiji Buddhist temple in Kyoto, Japan, a robot named Mindar is already offering sermons to the faithful. Mindar doesn't look like your usual robot; it's designed to look like Kannon, the Buddhist bodhisattva of compassion. As of yet, Mindar isn't controlled by AI; it gives pre-recorded advice and blessings while moving and gesturing as a human might. But the robot's designers aim to build AI-powered systems that will allow Mindar to provide appropriately tailored feedback for worshippers' needs. It's a small step from an AI serving as a priest in a traditional religion to an AI leading a novel one.

WOTF and similar ventures are extreme examples of possible new faiths. But such approaches will appeal to those who believe that big data and technology can offer answers to life's biggest questions. And there are, of course, other routes to reformulation. For example, the Mexican Santa Muerte movement, while incorporating aspects of Catholicism, centers on a new female saint, though she's treated more like a deity. As the name suggests, *Santa Muerte* or "Saint of Death" personifies divine energies associated with that most profound transition. She's usually depicted as a skeleton dressed in brightly colored robes and is believed to have both the power to heal and to assure a path to a heavenly afterlife. And while veneration of Santa Muerte has been around for a century or more, it suddenly started growing exponentially in 2001. With that explosive growth, now including more than ten million people, the symbolism and the rituals attached to Her have been changing as well.

For example, she's now often associated with symbols such as a scale and an hourglass. Whereas the former symbolizes equity and justice, as death can be seen as the great equalizer (no one is immune from it), the latter symbolizes that while time on earth is short, life can begin again in a new realm when the hourglass is flipped. The rituals associated with Santa Muerte are not standardized but often include elements taken from Santeria, Catholicism, and New Age–inspired ideas about spiritual energy that are remixed in novel ways. In this mix, people find fresh ways to pray and to make offerings to Santa Muerte in the hopes that she will improve their health and prosperity on earth or ease their way to life in the next realm.

Like so many of the rituals we've seen, the goal is strengthening beliefs that provide comfort while also building community. And while Santa Muerte has adherents throughout all social strata, her greatest appeal seems to be to those who are more economically distressed or traditionally marginalized in Mexico and Latin America: the urban working class, the LGBTQ community, and the poor. The faith's focus on themes of equality, of acceptance, and of a route to salvation (whether in this world or the next) resonates especially well with these groups.

Building an entirely new religion is a massive undertaking, however. And most new religions either don't last or, if they do hang around, don't grow much. While part of the reason is certainly due to the absence of a state sponsor—after all, in the old days, people often joined the religions that their rulers told them to join—there's another factor to consider: a religion has to work psychologically. It has to provide meaning. It has to move you. It has to feel right. Without that, it's not much different from a club. Whether new religions grow, then, depends on how nimbly they adapt their practices and rituals to the needs of people.

So if you're looking for a new route to spirituality, what do you do? My suggestion isn't to try starting a new religion but to follow the lead of organizations like the Sacred Design Lab (SDL) that creatively modify and apply ancient practices to emergent challenges. SDL was founded by three Harvard Ministry Innovation Fellows—Angie Thurston, Casper ter Kuile, and Sue Phillips—as a research and development lab focused on twenty-first-century spiritual well-being. They've worked with Google to examine how the changing dynamics of work might impact spiritual well-being, with the Obama Foundation to design a social action curriculum that provides deeper social connection, and with the Sundance Film Festival to think about digital placemaking and ritual. They also regularly consult with many religious organizations about ritual innovation.

What I most admire about SDL is that its philosophy is based on three pillars common to many major faiths. The first is *belonging*—the recognition that humans are happiest when we care, support, and show compassion for one another. The second is *becoming*—the realization that we need to find ways to develop and share our gifts, competencies, and expertise. To foster these goals, however, the good folks at SDL also recognize that it's helpful for people to feel a connection to something bigger—some sort of higher power or purpose. And that brings us to their third pillar: *beyond*—the belief that we are all bound up in something larger than ourselves. In one way or another, almost all the rituals and practices we've considered in this book touch on these pillars at different moments of life. They're panhuman needs and concerns, as evidenced by religion's ubiquity. But SDL adds something unique in its approach to constructing new spiritual technologies. Unlike other organizations or start-ups that create rituals on the fly, it studies hard and reaches back.

To design new rituals, SDL looks to traditional practices from all over the world that have been used to help people flourish for centuries. It then remixes them in thoughtful ways that it evaluates by trials with real people: experiments of sorts. This work is intensive. It's time-consuming. It requires a great deal of thought and motivation. But it's precisely because of this strategy that the results they produce are more likely to offer benefits. Different ways to use breath and bodily movements to build connection. Novel ways to worship together by applying aspects of Muslim chanting and synchronous praying to different forms of spirituality. And on it goes, with the goal in each case being the design of new rituals and practices that help people thrive in the face of challenges.

Coming Together

The one thing most social scientists, priests, imams, shamans, and rabbis share is a desire to help people live their best lives. To grow, to love, to find the joys that this world can bring while helping those less fortunate to do so too. But figuring out exactly how to do this in the most thoughtful and productive way possible will require collaboration between scientific and religious thinkers. Yes, there's been a little of that lately. Working together, scientists and Buddhist monks have identified and quantified the benefits of meditation and secularized its practice to make it available to all people, irrespective of faith. But there must be more out there to discover. Mindfulness isn't a fluke where religion just happened to get something right. As I said at the outset of our journey together, scientists need to be a bit humbler. Like some of our medical colleagues who bioprospect to find cures for people's physical ills, scientists need to religioprospect—to plumb the depths of religious practices to see how and why they can help people along life's path.

Through religioprospecting, physicians might find ways to be even more effective and comforting. Making time to take a few synchronous breaths together with patients in a simple, secular ritual should increase feelings of empathy and trust. In turn, those feelings should help medical therapies work better in some cases and, in stressful or painful situations like biopsies, also reduce patients' anxiety and discomfort. Setting times for simple gratitude rituals can help parents nudge honesty, generosity, and patience in their children (and in each other). Creating a daily schedule in which those struggling with grief perform actions (like simple physical exercises) that cause mild onsets and offsets of discomfort can be an additional strategy in a therapist's toolbox. Regularly setting aside time to remind ourselves via a simple ritual that death isn't as far off as we often think can help reorient our values away from selfish materialism and toward kindness and connection. These are only a few possibilities pulled from the technologies religions use. More of them certainly await us if we're willing to look.

Of course, collaboration goes both ways. Just as scientists can learn from religion, religious leaders can learn from science. By learning how rituals and practices influence the mind most effectively—which elements reduce anxiety, which build connection, which increase morality, which heal grief and pain—religious leaders can best help their followers adapt to trying situations, even novel ones. They can do so upfront, by looking to science for ideas about how to better target rituals to certain needs, or they can do it retrospectively, by using the tools of science to evaluate changes they made on the fly—like many of those necessitated by social distancing during the COVID-19 pandemic—met the needs of their flocks. Collaborations like these can also help religions adapt and leverage technological advancements. Religious leaders can discover new ways to conduct rituals over mobile devices. Shamans can find newer and safer ways to use or combine psychedelics to foster transcendence through targeting specific neural pathways—pathways that neuroscientists are only now starting to map.

I recognize that this type of collaborative knowledge seeking won't be easy at first. In many ways, it requires breaking down some of the most stubborn barriers in education that exist—barriers that can be found from grade schools to the greatest universities in the world. The debates continue to rage: evolution versus creationism, logic versus superstition. These barriers, like many in the social world, are buttressed by ideology. They separate people into camps that disparage one another. But if you remove the ideology, the barriers crumble. People begin to see one another as people, not as enemies.

While we shouldn't expect scientists to abandon empiricism or religious leaders to abandon theology, there's no reason why they can't work together to improve the human condition in the areas where they agree. Many religions run hospitals that use scientific technology to heal people; they don't just rely on prayer. Why not use science to study how faith practices can improve health and well-being too? Likewise, I've just cataloged throughout this book how science has "discovered" many tools that religions have been using for thousands of years to influence the mind. Why not look for more? I'd argue that choosing not to work together—not to use every tool that evolution or God gave us to help one another—is one of the greatest sins we might commit.

To collaborate in this way, we'll need to develop a new field of interdisciplinary inquiry—one that doesn't stand between two sides throwing rocks but rather has its feet firmly planted in two realms that have guided human advancement throughout history: science and religion. It's here that universities and research-funding agencies must take the lead. Together, they drive the pursuit of knowledge, and that means they have the power to keep the barriers in place or to tear them down. Thought leaders need to do the same by creating spaces in society for productive conversations instead of hubristic disparagement. It's not that scientists, religious leaders, people of every faith, and people of no faith need to agree on everything. Even among themselves, they surely don't. But we all must agree on the importance of intellectual humility and cooperation. It's through science and religion working together while respecting each other that we can find new ways to do "God's work" here on earth.

Acknowledgments

Writing a book is always a journey. And on this one, I've benefited immeasurably from my companions. First and foremost, I want to thank my wife, Amy, who wore many hats: editor, conversation partner, cheerleader, and critic. She helped me not only think more deeply about ideas but also communicate them more effectively. To put it mildly, she made this book (and my life) better in more ways than I can count! I'd also like to thank my two daughters. Their love served as a great source of support throughout this project.

I've also benefited from the insights of many friends and colleagues—too many to list and so I won't try. But here, two friends deserve special mention for the exceptional amounts of time they took to speak with me about this project. Jamie Ryerson helped me shape and refine my original insights into how and why science and religion should work together. And Rabbi Geoffrey Mitelman helped me understand not only more about the specifics of certain Jewish rituals but also why religious leaders should be open to scientific knowledge.

I'm eternally grateful to my agent, Jim Levine, who again helped me to work with editor par excellence Eamon Dolan, and also to Eamon himself for his interest in this project and his partnership in bringing it to fruition. When I say partnership, I mean

Acknowledgments

that in the truest sense of the word. Eamon contributed to every stage of the writing process. From helping to structure the original arguments, to adding his own insights and challenging mine, to pruning my habitual verbosity, Eamon's fingerprints are all over this book—a book that would not exist (or be as readable) if not for Eamon's guiding hand.

I also owe a debt to Northeastern University for supporting my research over the twenty years I've worked there, and to both the National Science Foundation and the John Templeton Foundation for grant funding that supported some of my lab's work described in this book.

Finally, I also want to thank the Center for Public Leadership at the Harvard Kennedy School for hosting me during a recent sabbatical that allowed me to write much of this book.

Notes

Introduction: The Journey Ahead

4 *Across the globe*: Pew Research Center, "Religion's Relationship to Happiness, Civic Engagement, and Health Around the World," Pew Forum, January 31, 2019, https://www.pewforum.org/2019/01/31/religions-relationship-to-happiness-civic-engagement-and-health-around-the-world/, accessed January 28, 2021.

5 *Even Richard Dawkins*: Al Webb, "Richard Dawkins Says He's Not Entirely Sure God Doesn't Exist," *Washington Post*, February 27, 2012, https://www.washingtonpost.com/national/on-faith/richard-dawkins-says-hes-not-entirely-sure-god-doesnt-exist/2012/02/24/gIQA7496XR_story.html, accessed January 28, 2021

6 *He even once said*: Tenzin Gyatso, "Our Faith in Science," *New York Times*, November 12, 2005, https://www.nytimes.com/2005/11/12/opinion/our-faith-in-science.html, accessed January 28, 2021.

8 *The best definition of "ritual"*: Catherine Bell, *Ritual Theory, Ritual Practice* (New York: Oxford University Press, 1992).

9 *In Silicon Valley*: Sigal Samuel, "A Design Lab Is Making Rituals for Secular People. Will it Work?" *Atlantic*, May 7, 2018, https://www.theatlantic.com/technology/archive/2018/05/ritual-design-lab-secular-atheist/559535/, accessed January 28, 2021.

9 *Recent experiments have shown*: A. D. Tian, J. Schroeder, G. Häubl, J. L. Risen, M. Norton, and F. Gino, "Enacting Rituals to Improve Self-Control," *Journal of Personality and Social Psychology* 114, no. 6 (2018): 851–76, doi: 10.1037/pspa0000113.

11 *It enhances attention*: Holger Cramer, Helen Hall, Matthew Leach, Jane Frawley, Yan Zhang, Brenda Leung, Jon Adams, and Romy Lauche, "Prevalence, Patterns, and Predictors of Meditation Use Among US Adults: A Nationally Representative Sample," *Scientific Reports* 6, no. 1 (2016): 36760, doi: 10.1038/srep36760. Madhav Goyal, Sonal Singh, and Erica M. S. Sibinga, "Meditation Programs for Psychological Stress and Wellbeing: A Systematic Review and Meta-Analysis," *JAMA Internal Medicine* 174, no. 3 (2014): 357–68, doi: 10.1001/jamainternmed.2013.13018. David DeSteno, "Compassion and Altruism: How Our Minds Determine Who Is Worthy of Help," *Current Opinion in Behavioral Sciences* 3 (2015): 80–83, doi: 10.1016/j.cobeha.2015.02.002.

12 *Through continued testing*: Chris Kilham, "Rosy Periwinkle: A Life Saving Plant," Fox News, July 31, 2013, https://www.foxnews.com/health/rosy-periwinkle-a-life-saving-plant, accessed January 28, 2021.

13 *More than 80 percent*: Pew Research Center, "The Global Religious Landscape," Pew Forum, December 18, 2012, https://www.pewforum.org/2012/12/18/global-religious-landscape-exec/, accessed January 28, 2021.

16 *having too many choices*: Sheena S. Iyengar and Mark R.

Lepper, "When Choice Is Demotivating," *Journal of Personality and Social Psychology* 79, no. 6 (2000): 995–1006, doi: 10.1037/002-3514.79.6.995.

16 *The psychologist Barry Schwartz*: Barry Schwartz, Andrew Ward, John Monterosso, Sonja Lyubomirsky, Katherine White, and Darrin R. Lehman, "Maximizing Versus Satisficing: Happiness Is a Matter of Choice," *Journal of Personality and Social Psychology* 83, no. 5 (2002): 1178–97, doi: 10.37//0022-3514.83.5.1178.

17 *believers showed less anxiety*: Michael Inzlicht, Ian McGregor, Jacob B. Hirsh, and Kyle Nash, "Neural Markers of Religious Conviction," *Psychological Science* 20, no. 3 (2009): 385–92, doi: 10.1111/j.1467-9280.2009.02305.x.

17 *In a similar vein*: Michael Inzlicht and Alexa M. Tullett, "Reflecting on God: Religious Primes Can Reduce Neurophysiological Response to Errors," *Psychological Science* 21, no. 8 (2010): 1184–90, doi: 10.1177/0956797610375451.

17 *links religious belief to decreased stress*: Kevin S. Seybold and Peter C. Hill, "The Role of Religion and Spirituality in Mental and Physical Health," *Current Directions in Psychological Science* 10, no. 1 (2001): 21–24, doi: 10.1111/1467-8721.00106.

18 *Loneliness is as dangerous*: William Harms, "AAAS 2014: Loneliness Is a Major Health Risk for Older Adults," University of Chicago News, February 16, 2014, https://news.uchicago.edu/article/2014/02/16/aaas-2014-loneliness-major-health-risk-older-adults, accessed January 28, 2021.

18 *It's precisely because*: Naomi Eisenberger, Matthew Lieberman, and Kipling Williams, "Does Rejection Hurt? An fMRI Study of Social Exclusion," *Science* 302, no. 5643 (2003): 290–92, doi: 10.1126/science.1089134.

18 *It's such a fundamental signal*: Christine Fawcett and Bahar Tuncgenc, "Infants' Use of Movement Synchrony to Infer

Social Affiliation in Others," *Journal of Experimental Child Psychology* 160 (2017): 127–36, doi: 10.1016/j.jecp.2017.03.014.

19 *One simple act*: Piercarlo Valdesolo and David DeSteno, "Synchrony and the Social Tuning of Compassion," *Emotion* 11, no. 2 (2011): 262–66, doi: 10.1037/a0021302.

19 *synchrony of any type*: Ronald Fischer, Rohan Callander, Paul Reddish, and Joseph Bulbulia, "How Do Rituals Affect Cooperation?" *Human Nature* 24 (2013): 115–25, doi: 10.1007/s12110-013-9167-y.

1: Infancy: Welcoming and Binding

28 *Via brain imaging*: Jeroen Vaes, Federica Meconi, Paola Sessa, and Mateusz Olechowski, "Minimal Humanity Cues Induce Neural Empathic Reactions Towards Non-Human Entities," *Neuropsychologia* 89 (2016): 132–40, doi: 10.1016/j.neuro psychologia.2016.06.004.

29 *Children who grow up without*: Elena Netsi, Rebecca M. Pearson, Lynne Murray, Peter Cooper, Michelle G. Craske, and Alan Stein, "Association of Persistent and Severe Postnatal Depression with Child Outcomes," *JAMA Psychiatry* 75, no. 3 (2018): 247–53, doi: 10.1001/jamapsychiatry.2017.4363.

30 *Fathers, too, get a hormone boost*: Ilanit Gordon, Orna Zagoory-Sharon, James Leckman, and Ruth Feldman, "Oxytocin and the Development of Parenting in Humans," *Biological Psychiatry* 68, no. 4 (2010): 377–82, doi: 10.1016/biopsych.2010.02.005.

30 *But, for some parents*: Josh Halliday, "One-Third of New Mothers Struggle to Bond with Their Baby, Research Shows," *Guardian,* June 5, 2016, https://www.theguardian.com/lifeand style/2016/jun/06/one-third-of-new-mothers-struggle-to-bond -with-their-baby-research-shows, accessed January 29, 2021.

30 *We don't care for children*: Alison Gopnik, *The Gardener and the Carpenter* (New York: Picador, 2016), p. 127.

31 *bias that affects social relationships*: Drake Baer, "The Fallacy That Keeps People in Unhappy Relationships," The Cut, https://www.thecut.com/2016/12/why-people-stay-in-unhappy-relationships.html, accessed January 29, 2021.

31 *Your mind's resistance*: Bjoern Hartig, "Two Wrongs Make a Right? Is the Sunk-Cost-Effect a Commitment Device Against Present Bias?" *SSRN,* August 21, 2017, doi: 10.2139/ssrn.3023700.

32 *cling harder to views*: Robert B. Cialdini and M. R. Trost, "Social Influence: Social Norms, Conformity and Compliance," in *The Handbook of Social Psychology (4th Edition),* eds. Daniel Gilbert, Susan T. Fiske, and Gardner Lindzey (Boston: McGraw-Hill, 1998).

32 *the bond between Japanese mothers*: Susan D. Holloway and Ayumi Nagase, "Child Rearing in Japan," in *Parenting Across Cultures: Childrearing, Motherhood and Fatherhood in Non-Western Cultures,* ed. H. Selin (Dordrecht: Springer, 2014).

33 *Japanese mothers do everything*: Fred Rothbaum, Martha Pott, Hiroshi Azuma, Kazuo Miyake, and John Weisz, "The Development of Close Relationships in Japan and the United States," *Child Development* 71, no. 5 (2000): 1121–42, doi: 10.1111/1467-8624.00214.

33 *These behaviors forge*: Ruth Feldman, "Parent-Infant Synchrony: Biological Foundations and Developmental Outcomes," *Current Directions in Psychological Science* 16, no. 6 (2007): 340–45, doi: 10.1111/j.1467-8721.2007.00532.x. Ashley M. Groh, R. M. Pasco Fearon, Marinus H. van Ijzendoorn, Martin J. Bakermans-Kranenburg, and Glenn I. Roisman, "Attachment in the Early Life Course: Meta-Analytic Evidence for

Its Role in Socioemotional Development," *Child Development Perspectives* 11, no. 1 (2017): 70–76, doi: 10.1111/cdep.12213.

33 *Cultures develop labels*: Lisa Feldman Barrett, *How Emotions Are Made* (New York: Houghton Mifflin Harcourt, 2017).

36 *about 12 percent of new mothers*: Shefaly Shorey, Cornelia Yin Ing Chee, Esperanza Debby Ng, Yiong Huak Chan, Wilson Wai San Tam, and Yap Seng Chong, "Prevalence and Incidence of Postpartum Depression Among Healthy Mothers: A Review and Meta-Analysis," *Journal of Psychiatric Research* 104 (2018): 235–48, doi: 10.1016/j.jpsychires.2018.08.001.

37 *poorer outcomes for children*: Elena Netsi, Rebecca M. Pearson, Lynne Murray, Peter Cooper, Michelle G. Craske, and Alan Stein, "Association of Persistent and Severe Postnatal Depression with Child Outcomes," *JAMA Psychiatry* 75, no. 5 (2018): 247–53, doi: 10.1001/jamapsychiatry.2017.4363.

38 *whether such confinement*: Rena Bina, "The Impact of Cultural Factors Upon Postpartum Depression," *Health Care for Women International* 29, no. 6 (2008): 568–92, doi: 10.1080/07399330802089149.

38 *study of 186 Taiwanese women*: Shu-Shya Heh, Lindsey Coombes, and Helen Bartlett, "The Association Between Depressive Symptoms and Social Support in Taiwanese Women During the Month," *International Journal of Nursing Studies* 41, no. 5 (2004): 573–79, doi: 10.1016/j.ijnurstu.2004.01.003.

38 *Similar findings come from*: Bina, "The Impact of Cultural Factors Upon Postpartum Depression."

38 *participating in religious activities*: Joshua R. Mann, Robert E. McKeown, Janice Bacon, Roumen Vesselinov, and Freda Bush, "Do Antenatal Religious and Spiritual Factors Impact the Risk of Postpartum Depressive Symptoms," *Journal of Women's Health* 17, no. 5 (2008): 745–55, doi: 10.1089/jwh.2007.0627.

38 *getting support from a community of friends*: Nancy Collins, Christine Dunkel-Schetter, Marci Lobel, and Susan C. Scrimshaw, "Social Support in Pregnancy: Psychosocial of Birth Outcomes and Postpartum Depression," *Journal of Personality and Social Psychology* 65, no. 6 (1993): 1243–58, doi: 10.1037//0022-3514.65.6.1243.

39 *A central reason why*: John Shaver, Chris G. Sibley, Richard Sosis, and Deane Galbraith, "Alloparenting and Religious Fertility: A Test of the Religious Alloparenting Hypothesis, *Evolution and Human Behavior* 40, no. 3 (2019): 315–24, doi: 10.1016/j.evolhumbehav.2019.01.004.

40 *Those whose accept*: Andrea D. Clements and Anna Ermakova, "Surrender to God and Stress: A Possible Link Between Religiosity and Health," *Psychology of Religion and Spirituality* 4, no. 2 (2012): 93–107, doi: 10.1037/a0025109.

40 *Pregnant women who*: Ibid. Andrea D. Clements, Tifani R. Fletcher, Lawrence D. Childress, Robert A. Montgomery, and Beth A. Bailey, "Social Support, Religious Commitment, and Depressive Symptoms in Pregnant and Postpartum Women," *Journal of Reproductive and Infant Psychology* 34, no. 3 (2016): 247–59, doi: 10.1080/02646838.2016.1152626.

40 *finding greater strength*: Alyssa C. D. Cheadle, Christine Dunkel Schetter, Robin Gaines Lanzi, Maxine Reed Vance, Latoya S. Sahadeo, Madeline U. Shalowitz, and the Community and Child Health Network, "Spiritual and Religious Resources in African American Women: Protection from Depressive Symptoms Following Birth," *Clinical Psychological Science* 3, no. 2 (2015): 283–91, doi: 10.1177/2167702614531581.

Notes

2: The Formative Years—
Learning What's Right and Wrong

45 *If we rank societies*: Ara Norenzayan, Azim F. Shariff, Will M. Gervais, Aiyana K. Willard, Rita A. McNamara, Edward Slingerland, and Joseph Henrich, "The Cultural Evolution of Prosocial Religions," *Behavioral and Brain Sciences* 39 (2016): e1, doi: 10.1017/S0140525X14001356.

45 *Henrich and his colleagues*: Benjamin Grant Purzycki, Coren Apicella, Quentin D. Atkinson, Emma Cohen, Rita Anne McNamara, Aiyana K. Willard, Dimitris Xygalatas, Ara Norenzayan, and Joseph Henrich, "Moralistic Gods, Supernatural Punishment and the Expansion of Human Sociality," *Nature* 530, no. 7590 (2016): 327–30, doi: 10.1038/nature16980.

46 *children as young as six*: Paul L. Harris and Melissa A. Koenig, "Trust in Testimony: How Children Learn About Science and Religion," *Child Development* 77, no. 3 (2006): 505–24, doi: 10.1111/j.1467-8624.2006.00886.x.

47 *By four years of age*: Kathleen H. Corriveau and Paul L. Harris, "Choosing Your Informant: Weighing Familiarity and Recent Accuracy," *Developmental Science* 12, no. 3 (2009): 426–37, doi: 10.1111/j.1467-7687.2008.00792.x.

47 *When you combine this fact*: Mark A. Sabbagh and Dare A. Baldwin, "Learning Words from Knowledgeable Versus Ignorant Speakers: Links Between Pre-Schoolers' Theory of Mind and Semantic Development," *Child Development* 72, no. 4 (2001): 1054–70, doi: 10.1111/1467-8624.00334.

49 *a little bit more credence*: Lisa K. Fazio, David G. Rand, and Gordon Pennycook, "Repetition Increases Perceived Truth Equally for Plausible and Implausible Statements," *Psychonomic Bulletin and Review* 26 (2019): 1705–1710, doi: 10.3758/

s13423-019-01651-4. Lisa K. Fazio, Raunak M. Pillai, and Deep Patel, "The Effects of Repetition on Belief in Naturalistic Settings," PsyArXiv, January 4, 2021, doi: 10.31234/osf.io/r85mw.

49 *holds true for children*: Lisa K. Fazio and Carrie L. Sherry, "The Effect of Repetition on Truth Judgements Across Development," *Psychological Science* 31, no. 9 (2020): 1150–60, doi: 10.1177/0956797620939534.

49 *the truer it rings*: Norbert Schwarz, "Metacognition," in *APA Handbook of Personality and Social Psychology*, vol. 1, eds. Mario Mikulincer, Philip R. Shaver, Eugene Borgida, and John A. Barth (Washington, DC: American Psychological Association, 2015), pp. 203–29.

50 *The theory of cognitive dissonance*: Leon Festinger, Henry Riecken, and Stanley Schacter, *When Prophecy Fails* (New York: Harper-Torchbooks, 1956).

51 *Numerous experiments have proven*: Joel Cooper, "Cognitive Dissonance Theory," in *Handbook of Theories of Social Psychology,* eds. Paul M. Van Lange, Arie W. Kruglanski, and E. Tory Higgins (Thousand Oaks, CA: Sage Publications, 2012).

52 *placed above other images*: Thomas W. Schubert, "Your Highness: Vertical Position as Perceptual Symbols of Power," *Journal of Personality and Social Psychology* 89, no. 1 (2005): 1–21, doi: 10.1037/0022-3514.89.1.1.

52–53 *positions below others*: Michael Niedeggen, Rudolf Kerschreiter, Diance Hirte, and Sarah Weschke, "Being Low Prepares for Being Neglected: Verticality Affects Expectancy of Social Participation," *Psychonomic Bulletin and Review* 24 (2017): 574–81, doi: 10.3758/s13423-016-1115-5.

53 *When they read information*: Tara Van Bommel, Alyssa Boasso, and Janet B. Ruscher, "Looking Up for Answers: Upward

Gaze Increases Receptivity to Advice," *Current Research in Social Psychology* 22, no. 11 (2014): 60–70, https://www.re searchgate.net/publication/288186888_Looking_up_for_an swers_Upward_gaze_increases_receptivity_to_advice.

53 *Hearing this information*: Gill Woodall and Judee K. Burgoon, "The Effects of Nonverbal Synchrony on Message Comprehension and Persuasiveness," *Journal of Nonverbal Behavior* 5 (1981): 207–223, doi: 10.1007/BF00987460.

55 *And this sense of connection*: Patty Van Cappellen, Vassilis Saroglou, and Maria Toth-Guathier, "Religiosity and Prosocial Behavior Among Churchgoers: Exploring Underlying Mechanisms," *International Journal for the Psychology of Religion* 26, no. 1 (2016): 19–30, doi: 10.1080/10508619.2014.958004.

56 *But among those who don't hold religious beliefs*: Victoria K. Alogna and Jamin Halberstadt, "The Divergent Effects of Prayer on Cheating," *Religion, Brain, and Behavior* 10, no. 4 (2020): 365–78, doi: 10.1080/2153599X.2019.1574881.

56 *If you lump all religious people together*: Wilhelm Hofmann, Daniel C. Wisneski, Mark J. Brandt, and Linda J. Skitka, "Morality in Everyday Life," *Science* 345, no. 6202 (2014): 1340–43, doi: 10.1126/science.1251560.

56 *Israelis who live*: Richard Sosis and Bradley J. Ruffle, "Religious Ritual and Cooperation: Testing for a Relationship on Israeli Religious and Secular Kibbutzim," *Current Anthropology* 44, no. 5 (2003): 713–22, doi: 10.1086/379260.

56 *Likewise, more devout Muslims*: Ali M. Ahmed, "Are Religious People More Prosocial? A Quasi-Experimental Study with 'Madrasah' Pupils in a Rural Community in India," *Journal for the Scientific Study of Religion* 48, no. 2 (2009): 368–74, https://www.jstor.org/stable/40405622.

56 *Christians are more generous*: Deepak Malhotra, "(When) Are Religious People Nicer? Religious Salience and the 'Sunday Effect' on Prosocial Behavior," *Judgment and Decision Making* 5, no. 2 (2010): 138–43, http://journal.sjdm.org/10/10216 /jdm10216.pdf. Benjamin Edelman, "Red Light States: Who Buys Online Adult Entertainment?" *Journal of Economic Perspectives* 23, no. 1 (2009): 209–220, http://www.benedelman.org /publications/redlightstates.pdf.

57 *Children younger than seven*: Nadia Chernyak, Kristin L. Leimgruber, Yarrow C. Dunham, Jingshi Hu, and Peter Blake, "Paying Back People Who Harmed Us but Not People Who Helped Us: Direct Negative Reciprocity Precedes Direct Positive Reciprocity in Early Development," *Psychological Science* 30, no. 9 (2019): 1273–86, doi: 10.1177/0956797619854975.

57 *And those who develop*: Peter Blake, Marco Piovesan, Natalia Montinari, Felix Warneken, "Prosocial Norms in the Classroom: The Role of Self-Regulation in Following Norms of Giving," *Journal of Economic Behavior and Organization* 115 (2015): 18–29, doi: 10.1016/j.jebo.2014.10.004.

57 *Research confirms that they'll give*: Erik P. Duhaime, "Is the Call to Prayer a Call to Cooperate? A Field Experiment on the Impact of Religious Salience on Prosocial Behavior," *Judgment and Decision Making* 10, no. 6 (2015): 593–96, http:// journal.sjdm.org/15/15623/jdm15623.pdf.

57 *Hindus who agreed to play*: Dimitris Xygalatas, "Effects of Religious Setting on Cooperative Behavior: A Case Study from Mauritius," *Religion, Brain, and Behavior* 3, no. 2 (2013): 91–102, doi: 10.1080/2153599X.2012.724547.

58 *People who had completed puzzles*: Azim F. Shariff and Ara Norenzayan, "God Is Watching You: Priming God Concepts

Increases Prosocial Behavior in an Anonymous Economic Game," *Psychological Science* 18, no. 9 (2007): 803–809, doi: 10.1111/j.1467-9280.2007.01983.x.

58 *prayer remains a way*: Robert A. Emmons, "Emotion and Religion," in *Handbook of the Psychology of Religion and Spirituality,* eds. Raymond F. Paloutzian and Crystal L. Park (New York: Guilford Press, 2005). Patty Van Cappellen, "Rethinking Self-Transcendent Positive Emotions and Religion: Insights from Psychological and Biblical Research," *Psychology of Religion and Spirituality* 9, no. 3 (2017): 254–63, doi: 10.1037 /rel0000101.

58 *Teens cite feeling grateful*: Gordon W. Allport, James M. Gillespie, and Jacqueline Young, "The Religion of the Post-War College Student," *Journal of Psychology: Interdisciplinary and Applied* 25, no. 1 (1948): 3–33, doi: 10.1080/0022 3980.1948.9917361.

59 *people who were randomly assigned to pray*: Nathaniel M. Lambert, Frank Fincham, Scott R. Braithwaite, Steven M. Graham, and Steven Beach, "Can Prayer Increase Gratitude?" *Psychology of Religion and Spirituality* 1, no. 3 (2009): 139–49, doi: 10.1037/a0016731.

59 *In my own research*: David DeSteno, Ye Li, Leah Dickens, and Jennifer S. Lerner, "Gratitude: A Tool for Reducing Economic Impatience," *Psychological Science* 25, no. 6 (2014): 1262–67, doi: 10.1177/0956797614529979.

59 *I also find*: David DeSteno, Fred Duong, Daniel Lim, and Shanyu Kates, "The Grateful Don't Cheat: Gratitude as a Fount of Virtue," *Psychological Science* 30, no. 7 (2019): 979–88, doi: 10.1177/0956797619848351.

59 *people are made to feel awe*: Piercarlo Valdesolo and Jesse Graham, "Awe, Uncertainty, and Agency Detection," *Psycholog-*

ical Science 25, no. 1 (2014): 170–78, doi: 10.1177/09567976
13501884.

59 *Other research shows*: Paul K. Piff, Pia Dietze, Matthew Feinberg, Daniel M. Stancato, and Dacher Keltner, "Awe, the Small Self, and Prosocial Behavior, *Journal of Personality and Social Psychology* 108, no. 6 (2015): 883–99, doi: 10.1037/pspi0000018.

60 *What's common to all these spaces*: Yannick Joye and Jan Verpooten, "An Exploration of the Functions of Religious Monumental Architecture from a Darwinian Perspective," *Review of General Psychology* 17, no. 1 (2013): 53–68, doi: 10.1037/a0029920.

61 *hearing these noble stories*: Karl Aquino, Brent McFerran, and Marjorie Laven, "Moral Identity and the Experience of Moral Elevation in Response to Acts of Uncommon Goodness," *Journal of Personality and Social Psychology* 100, no. 4 (2011): 703–718, doi: 10.1037/a0022540. Simone Schnall and Jean Roper, "Elevation Puts Moral Values into Action," *Social Psychological and Personality Science* 3, no. 3 (2012): 373–78, doi: 10.1177/1948550611423595.

61 *As Richard Thaler and Cass Sunstein*: Richard H. Thaler and Cass R. Sunstein, *Nudge* (New Haven, CT: Yale University Press, 2008).

61 *people who owe back taxes*: Michael Hallsworth, John A. List, Robert D. Metcalfe, and Ivo Vlaev, "The Behavioralist as Tax Collector: Using Natural Field Experiments to Enhance Tax Compliance," *Journal of Public Economics* 148 (2017): 14–31, doi: 10.1016/j.jpubeco.2017.02.003.

64 *But the strength of this preference*: Nicole J. Wen, Patricia A. Hermann, and Cristine H. Legare, "Ritual Increases Children's Affiliation with In-Group Members," *Evolution and Human Behavior* 37, no. 1 (2016): 54–60, doi: 10.1016/j.evolhumbehav.2015.08.002.

3: Coming of Age—Adulting Isn't Easy

72 *automatically tag them as less trustworthy*: Francesca Righetti and Catrin Finkenauer, "If You Are Able to Control Yourself, I Will Trust You: The Role of Perceived Self-Control in Interpersonal Trust," *Journal of Personality and Social Psychology* 100, no. 5 (2011): 874–86, doi: 10.1037/a0021827.

72 *in the Pygmalion effect*: Robert Rosenthal and Lenore Jacobson, "Pygmalion in the Classroom," *Urban Review* 3 (1968): 16–20, https://link.springer.com/article/10.1007/BF02322211. While this finding attracted a lot of astonishment and criticism at first, follow-up work on over 345 additional investigations has supported the existence of a Pygmalion effect, the magnitude of which is moderated by social conditions: Lee Jussim and Kent Harber, "Teacher Expectations and Self-Fulfilling Prophecies: Known and Unknowns, Resolved and Unresolved Controversies," *Personality and Social Psychology Review* 9, no. 2 (2005): 131–55, doi: 10.1207/s15327957 pspr0902_3.

73 *Mothers' expectations*: Stephanie Madon, Max Guyll, Richard L. Spoth, Susan E. Cross, and Sarah Hilbert, "The Self-Fulfilling Influence of Mother Expectations on Children's Underage Drinking," *Journal of Personality and Social Psychology* 84, no. 6 (2003): 1188–1205, doi: 10.1037/0022 -3514.84.6.1188.

73 *If people expect another person*: Stephanie Madon, Lee Jussim, Max Guyll, Heather Nofziger, Elizabeth R. Salib, Jennifer Willard, and Kyle C. Scherr, "The Accumulation of Stereotype-Based Self-Fulfilling Prophecies," *Journal of Personality and Social Psychology* 115, no. 5 (2018): 825–44, doi: 10.1037/psp i0000142.

76 *As Xygalatas's description*: Dimitris Xygalatas, "Trial by Fire," Aeon, September 19, 2014, https://aeon.co/essays/how-extreme-rituals-forge-intense-social-bonds, accessed January 31, 2021.

77 *Xygalatas found a bodily linkage*: Ibid. See also Carl D. Marci, Jacob Ham, Erin Moran, and Scott P. Orr, "Physiologic Correlates of Perceived Therapist Empathy and Social-Emotional Process During Psychotherapy," *Journal of Nervous Mental Disorders* 195, no. 2 (2007): 103–11, doi: 10.1097/01.nmd.0000253731.71025.fc.

78 *as the importance of knowledge*: Hayyim Schauss, "History of Bar Mitzvah," My Jewish Learning, https://www.myjewishlearning.com/article/history-of-bar-mitzvah/, accessed January 31, 2021. Suri Levow Krieger, "Bar and Bat Mitzvah: History and Practice," Academy for Jewish Religion, https://ajr.edu/5765journal/krieger5765/, accessed January 31, 2021.

82 *Our frontal lobes*: B. J. Casey, Rebecca M. Jones, Todd A. Hare, "The Adolescent Brain," *Annals of the New York Academy of Sciences* 1124 (2008): 111–26, doi: 10.1196/annals.1440.010.

82 *newest understanding of brain development*: Juliet Y. Davidow, Karin Foerde, Adriana Galvan, and Daphna Shohamy, "An Upside to Reward Sensitivity: The Hippocampus Supports Enhanced Reinforcement Learning in Adolescence," *Neuron* 92, no. 1 (2016): 93–99, doi: 10.1016/j.neuron.2016.08.031.

85 *Many employers*: Knight-Ridder/Tribune, "Experts Say Eagle Scouts Fly Highest in Job Hunt," *Chicago Tribune*, June 4, 1995, https://www.chicagotribune.com/news/ct-xpm-1995-06-04-9506040375-story.html, accessed January 31, 2021.

4: Transcending the Twenties and Thirties— Love, Connection, and (Maybe) Ecstasy

89   *"With my body I honor you"*: The Church of England, "Marriage," The Church of England, https://www.churchofengland .org/prayer-and-worship/worship-texts-and-resources/com mon-worship/marriage#mm095, accessed January 31, 2021.

89   *"Let him kiss me"*: Song of Songs (KJV) 1: 2–4.

92   *In children*: Susan D. Calkins and Susan P. Keane, "Cardiac Vagal Regulation Across the Preschool Period: Stability, Continuity, and Implications for Childhood Adjustment," *Developmental Psychobiology* 45, no. 3 (2004): 101–112, doi: 10.1002 /dev.20020.

92   *In adults*: Bethany E. Kok and Barbara L. Fredrickson, "Upward Spirals of the Heart: Autonomic Flexibility, as Indexed by Vagal Tone, Reciprocally and Prospectively Predicts Positive Emotions and Social Connectedness," *Biological Psychology* 85, no. 3 (2010): 432–36, doi: 10.1016/j.biopsy cho.2010.09.005. Christopher Oveis, Adam B. Cohen, June Gruber, Michelle N. Shiota, Jonathan Haidt, and Dacher Keltner, "Resting Respiratory Sinus Arrhythmia Is Associated with Tonic Positive Emotionality," *Emotion* 9, no. 2 (2009): 265–70, doi: 10.1037/a0015383.

92   *And in the case of romantic love*: Inna Schneiderman, Yael Zilberstein-Kra, James F. Leckman, and Ruth Feldman, "Love Alters Autonomic Reactivity to Emotions," *Emotion* 11, no. 6 (2011): 1314–21, doi: 10.1037/a0024090.

93   *Their breathing and heart rates*: Richard V. Palumbo, Marissa E. Marraccini, Lisa L. Weyandt, Oliver Wilder-Smith, Heather A. McGee, Siwei Liu, and Matthew S. Goodwin, "Interpersonal Autonomic Physiology: A Systematic Review

of the Literature," *Personality and Social Psychology Review* 21, no. 2 (2017): 99–141, doi: 10.1177/1088868316628405.

93 *Synchrony helps intuition*: Leonie Koban, Anand Ramamoorthy, Ivana Konvalinka, "Why Do We Fall into Sync With Others? Interpersonal Synchronization and the Brain's Optimization Principle," *Social Neuroscience* 14, no. 1 (2019): 1–9, doi: 10.1080/17470919.2017.1400463.

93 *The happier they are*: Jonathan L. Helm, David A. Sbarra, and Emilio Ferrer, "Coregulation of Respiratory Sinus Arrhythmia in Adult Romantic Partners," *Emotion* 14, no. 3 (2014): 522–31, doi: 10.1037/a0035960.

94 *Sustained rhythmic, physical stimulation*: Adam Safron, "What Is Orgasm? A Model of Sexual Trance and Climax via Rhythmic Entrainment," *Socioaffective Neuroscience & Psychology* 6, no. 1 (2016), doi: 10.3402/snp.v6.31763.

96 *Saint Teresa's description*: St. Teresa of Avila, *The Life of Saint Teresa of Jesus,* trans. David Lewis (New York: Benziger Brothers, 1904), 165–66.

98 *Twenty-five percent*: Marco Schlosser, Terje Sparby, Sebastjan Vörös, Rebecca Jones, and Natalie L. Marchant, "Unpleasant Meditation-Related Experiences in Regular Meditators: Prevalence, Predictors, and Conceptual Considerations," *PLoS One* 14, no. 5 (2019): e0216643, doi: 10.1371/journal.pone.0216643.

98 *While some of these instances*: Thomas Rocha, "The Dark Knight of the Soul," *Atlantic*, June 25, 2014, https://www.theatlantic.com/health/archive/2014/06/the-dark-knight-of-the-souls/372766/, accessed February 1, 2021.

100 *Both of these actions*: Stephen W. Porges, "Vagal Pathways: Portals to Compassion," in *The Oxford Handbook of Compassion Science,* eds. Emma M. Seppälä, Emiliana Simon-Thomas,

Stephanie L. Brown, Monica C. Worline, C. Daryl Cameron, and James R. Doty (New York: Oxford University Press, 2017), 189–202.

100 *consequence of meditation*: Blaine Ditto, Marie Eclache, and Natalie Goldman, "Short-Term Autonomic and Cardiovascular Effects of Mindfulness Body Scan Meditation," *Annals of Behavioral Medicine* 32 (2006): 227–34, doi: 10.1207/s15324796abm3203_9. Bethany E. Kok, Kimberly A. Coffey, Michael A. Cohen, Lahnna I. Catalino, Tanya Vacharkulksemsuk, Sara B. Algoe, Mary Brantley, and Barbara L. Fredrickson, "How Positive Emotions Build Physical Health: Perceived Positive Social Connections Account for the Upward Spiral Between Positive Emotions and Vagal Tone, *Psychological Science* 24, no. 7 (2013): 1123–32, doi: 10.1177/0956797612470827.

100 *When researchers compared*: Luciano Bernardi, Peter Sleight, Gabriele Bandinelli, Simone Cencetti, Lamberto Fattorini, Johanna Wdowczyc-Szulc, and Alfonso Lagi, "Effect of Rosary Prayer and Yoga Mantras on Autonomic Cardiovascular Rhythms: Comparative Study," *BMJ* 323, no. 73 (2001): 1446–49, doi: 10.1136/bmj.323.7327.1466.

101 *synchronized as they sing*: Victor Müller and Ulman Lindenberger, "Cardiac and Respiratory Patterns Synchronize Between Persons During Choir Singing," *PLoS One* 6, no. 9 (2011): e24893, doi: 10.1371/journal.pone.0024893.

102 *monastic design exploits*: Porges, "Vagal Pathways: Portals to Compassion," 199–200.

102 *default mode network*: Kathleen A. Garrison, Thomas A. Zeffiro, Dustin Scheinost, R. Todd Constable, and Judson A. Brewer, "Meditation Leads to Reduced Default Mode Network Activity Beyond an Active Task," *Cognitive, Affective,*

and Behavioral Neuroscience 15 (2015): 712–20, doi: 10.3758 /s13415-015-0358-3.

103 *During meditation*: Judson A. Brewer, Patrick D. Worhunsky, Jeremy R. Gray, Yi-Yuan Tang, Jochen Weber, and Hedy Kober, "Meditation Experience Is Associated with Differences in Default Mode Network Activity and Connectivity," *Proceedings of the National Academy of Sciences* 108, no. 50 (2011): 20254–59, doi: 10.1073/pnas.1112029108.

103 *While the rhythmic chanting*: Christopher Manoharan and Dimitris Xygalatas, "How Hearts Align in a Muslim Ritual," Sapiens, August 15, 2019, https://www.sapiens.org/biology/sufi -ritual-istanbul/, accessed February 1, 2021.

103 *brains of Sufis*: Yusuf O. Cakmak, Gazanfer Ekinci, Armin Heinecke, and Safiye Çavdar, "A Possible Role of Prolonged Whirling Episodes on Structural Plasticity of the Cortical Networks and Altered Vertigo Perception: The Cortex of Sufi Whirling Dervishes," *Frontiers of Human Neuroscience*, January 23, 2017, doi: 10.3389/fnhum.2017.00003.

103 *By placing the body*: Anupama Tyagi and Marc Cohen, "Yoga and Heart Rate Variability: A Comprehensive Review of the Literature," *International Journal of Yoga* 9, no. 2 (2016): 97–113, https://www.ijoy.org.in/article.asp?issn=0973 -6131;year=2016;volume=9;issue=2;spage=97;epage=113;aulast =Tyagi.

105 *Sean Illing*: Sean Illing, "The Brutal Mirror: What the Psychedelic Drug Ayahuasca Showed Me About My Life," Vox, November 12, 2019, https://www.vox.com/first-person/2018 /2/19/16739386/ayahuasca-retreat-psychedelic-hallucination -meditation, accessed February 1, 2021.

106 *heightened state of mindfulness*: Frederic Sampedro et al., "Assessing the Psychedelic 'After-Glow' in Ayahuasca Users:

Post-Acute Neurometabolic Function Connectivity Changes Are Associated with Enhanced Mindfulness Capacities," *International Journal of Psychoneuropharmacology* 20, no. 9 (2017): 698–711, doi: 10.1093/ijnp/pyx036.

107 *In 2006*: Roland Griffiths, W. A. Richards, U. McCann, and R. Jesse, "Psilocybin Can Occasion Mystical-Type Experiences Having Substantial and Sustained Personal Meaning and Spiritual Significance," *Psychopharmacology* 187, no. 3 (2006): 268–83, doi: 10.1007/s00213-006-0457-5.

108 *In fact, psilocybin use*: Katherine A. MacLean, Matthew W. Johnson, and Roland Griffiths, "Mystical Experiences Occasioned by the Hallucinogen Psilocybin Lead to Increases in the Personality Domain of Openness," *Journal of Psychopharmacology* 25, no. 11 (2011): 1453–61, doi: 10.1177/0269881111420188.

108 *Like ayahuasca, though*: "Q&A with Study Authors Roland Griffiths and Robert Jesse on 'Bad Trips,'" Johns Hopkins News and Publications, https://www.hopkinsmedicine.org /news/media/qanda_griffiths.html, accessed February 1, 2021. Bheatrix Bienemann, Nina Stamato Ruschel, Maria Luiza Campos, Marco Auréllio Negreiros, and Daniel C. Mograbi, "Self-Reported Negative Outcomes of Psilocybin Users: A Qualitative Analysis," *PLoS One* 15, no. 2 (2020): e0229067.

109 *Sufi master Rumi*: Rumi, "Rumi: Rumi Quotes and Poems," Rumi.org, https://www.rumi.org.uk, accessed February 1, 2021.

109 *Many non-Hindus*: Douglass Todd, "Christian Sex Is Better than Tantric Sex, Says Researcher," *Vancouver Sun*, July 26, 2008, https://vancouversun.com/news/staff-blogs/christian-sex -is-better-than-tantric-sex-says-researcher, accessed February 1, 2021.

109 *Even Albert Einstein*: "Mysticism and Reason," Britannica,

https://www.britannica.com/topic/mysticism/Mysticism-and
-reason, accessed February 1, 2021.

109 *As Michael Pollan*: Michael Pollan, "Not So Fast on Psychedelic Mushrooms," *New York Times*, May 10, 2019, https://www.nytimes.com/2019/05/10/opinion/denver-mushrooms-psilocybin.html, accessed February 1, 2021.

110 *Yet, in its traditional form*: Cendri A. Hutcherson, Emma M. Seppala, and James J. Gross, "Loving-Kindness Meditation Increases Social Connectedness," *Emotion* 8, no. 5 (2008): 720–24, doi: 10.1037/a0013237.

111 *In his most recent work*: Richard Schiffman, "Psilocybin: A Journey Beyond the Fear of Death?" *Scientific American*, December 1, 2016, https://www.scientificamerican.com/article/psilocybin-a-journey-beyond-the-fear-of-death/, accessed February 1, 2021.

5: The Business of Midlife I— Maintenance for the Body

113 *While 26 percent of people*: National Center for Health Statistics, "More than One-Third of U.S. Adults Use Complementary and Alternative Medicine According to New Government Survey," Center for Disease Control and Prevention, May 27, 2004, https://www.cdc.gov/nchs/pressroom/04news/adultsmedicine.htm, accessed February 2, 2021.

113 *During the 2020 COVID-19 outbreak*: Pew Research Center, "Most Americans Say Coronavirus Outbreak Has Impacted Their Lives," Pew Social Trends, March 30, 2020, https://www.pewsocialtrends.org/2020/03/30/most-americans-say-coronavirus-outbreak-has-impacted-their-lives/, accessed February 2, 2021.

114 *Eighty-five percent of people*: Jeff Levin, "Prevalence and Religious Predictors of Healing Prayer Use in the USA: Findings from the Baylor Religion Survey," *Journal of Religion and Health* 55, no. 4 (2016): 1136–58, doi: 10.1007/s10943-016 -0240-9.

116 *Pew Research Center*: Pew Research Center, "Religion's Relationship to Happiness, Civic Engagement, and Health Around the World," Pew Forum, January 31, 2019, https://www.pew forum.org/2019/01/31/religions-relationship-to-happiness-civic -engagement-and-health-around-the-world/, accessed February 2, 2021.

117 *In 2001, the Mayo Clinic*: Paul S. Mueller, David Plevak, Teresa A. Rummans, "Religious Involvement, Spirituality, and Medicine: Implications for Clinical Practice," *Mayo Clinic Proceedings* 76, no. 12 (2001): 1225–35, doi: 10.4065/76.12.1225.

119 *use positive religious coping strategies*: Nalini Tarakeshwar, Lauren C. Vanderwerker, Elizabeth Paulk, Michelle J. Pearce, Stanislav V. Kasi, and Holly G. Prigerson, "Religious Coping Is Associated with the Quality of Life of Patients with Advanced Cancer," *Journal of Palliative Medicine* 9, no. 3 (2006): 646–57, doi: 10.1089/jpm.2006.9.646.

119 *look at other chronic illnesses*: Dale A. Matthews, Michael E. McCullough, David B. Larson, Harold G. Koenig, James P. Swyers, and Mary Greenwold Milano, "Religious Commitment and Health Status: A Review of the Research and Implications for Family Medicine," *Archives of Family Medicine* 7, no. 2 (1998): 118–24, doi: 10.1001/archfami.7.2.118.

120 *smoke less, drink less, and avoid substance abuse*: Pew Research Center. Mueller et al., "Religious Involvement, Spirituality, and Medicine: Implications for Clinical Practice."

120 *see a physician for preventive care*: George W. Comstock and

Kay B. Partridge, "Church Attendance and Health," *Journal of Chronic Diseases* 25, no. 12 (1972): 665–72, doi: 10.1016/0021 -9681(72)90002-1.

120 *Judaism's Talmud*: *Talmud,* Sanhedrin 17b.

120 *quality of life will suffer*: Tarakeshwar et al., "Religious Coping is Associated with the Quality of Life."

121 *American Enterprise Institute found*: Daniel A. Cox, Ryan Streeter, and David Wilde, "A Loneliness Epidemic? How Marriage, Religion, and Mobility Explain the Generation Gap in Loneliness," American Enterprise Institute, September 26, 2019, https://www.aei.org/research-products/report/loneliness -epidemic-how-marriage-religion-and-mobility-explain -the-generation-gap-in-loneliness/, accessed February 3, 2021.

122 *A large study by the National Social Life, Health, and Aging Project*: Sunshine Rote, Terrence D. Hill, and Christopher G. Ellison, "Religious Attendance and Loneliness in Later Life," *Gerontologist* 53, no. 1 (2013): 39–50, doi: 10.1093/geront/gn s063.

123 *What Wolf found*: Stewart Wolf and John G. Bruhn, *The Power of the Clan: The Influence of Human Relationships on Heart Disease* (New York: Routledge, 1998).

124 *There was one big difference*: Ron Grossman and Charles Leroux, "A New 'Roseto Effect,'" *Chicago Tribune*, October 11, 1996, https://www.chicagotribune.com/news/ct-xpm-1996-10 -11-9610110254-story.html, accessed February 3, 2021.

124 *Wolf and Bruhn concluded*: John G. Bruhn and Stewart Wolf, *The Roseto Story: An Anatomy of Health* (Norman: University of Oklahoma Press, 2003).

128 *But physicians have long used*: Anton J. M. de Craen, Ted J. Kaptchuk, Jan G. P. Tijssen, and J. Kleijnen, "Placebos and Placebo Effects in Medicine: Historical Overview," *Journal*

of the Royal Society of Medicine 92, no. 10 (1999): 511–15, doi: 10.1177/014107689909201005.

128 *They've been shown to produce*: Damien G. Finniss, Ted J. Kaptchuk, Franklin Miller, and Fabrizio Benedetti, "Biological, Clinical, and Ethical Advances of Placebo Effects," *Lancet* 375, no. 9715 (2010): 686–95, doi: 10.1016/S0140 -6736(09)61706-2.

129 *scientists from the University of Maryland*: Fabrizio Benedetti et al., "Placebo-Responsive Parkinson Patients Show Decreased Activity in Single Neurons of Subthalamic Nucleus," *Nature Neuroscience* 7 (2004): 587–88, doi: 10.1038/nn1250.

130 *review of placebo surgery studies*: Karolina Wartolowska et al., "Use of Placebo Controls in the Evaluation of Surgery: Systematic Review," *BMJ* 348 (2014): g3253, doi: 10.1136/bmj .g3253.

131 *Even though the level of heat*: Pin-Hao A. Chen, Jin Hyun Cheong, Eshin Jolly, Hirsh Elhence, Tor D. Wager, and Luke J. Chang, "Socially Transmitted Placebo Effects," *Nature Human Behaviour* 3 (2019): 1295–1305, doi: 10.1038/s41562-019-0749-5.

132 *research using open-label placebos*: Ted J. Kaptchuk and Franklin G. Miller, "Placebo Effects in Medicine," *New England Journal of Medicine* 373 (2015): 8–9, doi: 10.1056/NEJMp1504023.

132 *significant reduction in IBS symptoms*: Ted J. Kaptchuk et al., "Placebos Without Deception: A Randomized Control Trial in Irritable Bowel Syndrome," *PLoS One* 5, no. 12 (2010): e15591, doi: 10.1371/journal.pone.0015591.

133 *Those who felt comfortable*: Kari A. Leibowitz, Emerson J. Hardebeck, J. Parker Goyer, and Alia J. Crum, "The Role of Patient Beliefs in Open-Label Placebo Effects," *Health Psychology* 38, no. 7 (2019): 613–22, doi: 10.1037/hea0000751.

135 *The result is*: S. Helen Ma and John D. Teasdale, "Mindfulness-Based Cognitive Therapy for Depression: Replication and Exploration of Different Relapse Prevention Effects," *Journal of Consulting and Clinical Psychology* 72, no. 1 (2004): 31–40, doi: 10.1037/0022-006X.72.1.31. J. David Creswell "Mindfulness-Based Stress Reduction Training Reduces Loneliness and Pro-Inflammatory Gene Expression in Older Adults: A Small Randomized Control Trial," *Brain Behavior and Immunity* 26, no. 7 (2012): 1095–1101, doi: 10.1016/j.bbi.2012.07.006.

136 *As she expected, Kober found*: Hedy Kober, Jason Buhle, Kevin N. Ochsner, and Tor D. Wager, "Let It Be: Mindful Acceptance Down-Regulates Pain and Negative Emotion," *Social Cognitive and Affective Neuroscience* 14, no. 11 (2019): 1147–58, doi: 10.1093/scan/nsz104.

138 *In an interview with Voice of America*: Cecily Hilleary, "Veterans with PTSD Find Relief in Native American Rituals," Voice of America, March 22, 2018, https://www.voanews.com /usa/veterans-ptsd-find-relief-native-american-rituals, accessed February 4, 2021.

138 *While there aren't yet any official statistics*: Ibid. Adam Ashton, "Veterans Find Peace, Purification at American Lake Sweat Lodge in Lakewood," *Tacoma News Tribune*, November 10, 2014, https://www.thenewstribune.com/news/local/military /article25892914.html, accessed February 4, 2021.

139 *although meditation is often beneficial*: Ausias Cebolla, Marcelo Demarzo, Patricia Martins, Joaquim Soler, and Javier Garcia-Campayo, "Unwanted Effects: Is There a Negative Side of Meditation? A Multicentre Survey," *PLoS One* 12, no. 9 (2017): e0183137, doi: 10.1371/journal.pone.0183137. Thomas Rocha, "The Dark Knight of the Soul," *Atlantic,* June

25, 2014, https://www.theatlantic.com/health/archive/2014/06
/the-dark-knight-of-the-souls/372766/, accessed February 1,
2021.

6: The Business of Midlife II— Maintenance for the Soul

142 *continuing to pursue a career*: Arthur C. Brooks, "Your Professional Decline Is Coming (Much) Sooner That You Think,"
Atlantic, July 2019, https://www.theatlantic.com/magazine
/archive/2019/07/work-peak-professional-decline/590650/,
accessed February 4, 2021.

143 *a U-shaped curve*: David G. Blanchflower and Andrew J. Oswald, "Is Well-Being U-Shaped over the Life Cycle?," *Social
Science and Medicine* 66, no. 8 (2008): 1733–49, doi: 10.1016/j
.socscimed.2008.01.030.

143 *Data from twenty-seven European nations*: David G. Blanchflower and Andrew J. Oswald, "Antidepressants and Age: A
New Form of Evidence for U-Shaped Well-Being Through
Life," *Journal of Economic Behavior and Organization* 127
(2016): 46–58, doi: 10.1016/j.jebo.2016.04.010.

143 *David Brooks describes*: David Brooks, *The Second Mountain*
(New York: Random House, 2019), p. 19.

144 *emphasis Jews place on most religious holidays*: Daniel Cox and
Robert P. Jones, "Chosen for What? Jewish Values in 2012,"
Public Religion Research Institute, April 3, 2012, https://www
.prri.org/research/jewish-values-in-2012/, accessed February
4, 2021.

145 *the percentage of those who regularly meditate*: Pew Research
"Frequency of Meditation by Age Group," Pew Forum, https://
www.pewforum.org/religious-landscape-study/compare/fre

quency-of-meditation/by/age-distribution/, accessed February 4, 2021.

148 *Buddhist teacher Atisha suggested*: John Powers, *Introduction to Tibetan Buddhism* (Boulder: Snow Lion, 2007), Chapter 10.

148 *Nine Contemplations of Atisha*: Joan Halifax Roshi, "The Nine Contemplations of Atisha," Upaya, https://www.upaya.org /dox/Contemplations.pdf, accessed February 4, 2021.

149 *Her data shows*: Laura L. Carstensen, "The Influence of a Sense of Time on Human Development," *Science* 312, no. 5782 (2006): 1913–15, doi: 10.1126/science.1127488.

149 *their values suddenly changed*: Ibid.

149 *Carstensen's team asked older people*: Ibid.

150 *only one of these strategies works*: Brett Q. Ford et al., "Culture Shapes Whether the Pursuit of Happiness Predicts Higher or Lower Well-Being," *Journal of Experimental Psychology: General* 144, no. 6 (2015): 1053–62, doi: 10.1037/xge0000108.

151 *So when experiments show*: Qiao Chu, Daniel Grühn, and Ashley M. Holland, "Before I Die: The Impact of Time Horizon and Age on Bucket-List Goals," *Journal of Gerontopsychology and Geriatric Psychiatry* 31, no. 3 (2018): 151–62, doi: 10.1024/1662-9647/a000190.

152 *The Talmud describes*: Talmud, Rosh Hashanah 16b, 32b.

153 *So our minds whitewash memories*: Maryam Kouchaki and Francesca Gino, "Memories of Unethical Actions Become Obfuscated Over Time," *Proceedings of the National Academy of Sciences* 113, no. 22 (2016): 6166–71, doi: 10.1073 /pnas.1523586113.

156 *That's a huge difference*: Paul Condon, Gaëlle Desbordes, Willa B. Miller, and David DeSteno, "Meditation Increases Compassionate Responses to Suffering," *Psychological Science* 24, no. 10 (2013): 2125–27, doi: 10.1177/0956797613485603.

156 *To be sure*: Daniel Lim, Paul Condon, and David DeSteno, "Mindfulness and Compassion: An Examination of Mechanism and Scalability," *PLoS One* 10, no. 2 (2015): e0118221, doi: 10.1371/journal.pone.0118221.

156 *to inflict some mild physical pain*: David DeSteno, Daniel Lim, Fred Duong, and Paul Condon, "Meditation Inhibits Aggressive Responses to Provocations," *Mindfulness* 9, no. 4 (2018): 1117–22, doi: 10.1007/s12671-017-0847-2.

156–57 *But when you combine our findings*: Helen Y. Weng et al., "Compassion Training Alters Altruism and Neural Responses to Suffering," *Psychological Science* 24, no. 7 (2013): 1171–80, doi: 10.1177/0956797612469537.

157 *The Meghiya Sutta*: Norman Fischer, "Making Friends on the Buddhist Path," Lion's Roar, May 12, 2017, https://www.lionsroar.com/friends-buddhist-path/, accessed February 4, 2021.

157 *minds turn toward social concerns*: Helene H. Fung, Minjie Lu, and Derek M. Isaacowitz, "Aging and Attention: Meaningfulness May Be More Important Than Valence," *Psychology and Aging* 34, no. 1 (2019): 85–90, doi: 10.1037/pag0000304.

7: Saying Goodbye—All that Lives Must Die

159 *the brain interprets separation*: Alan Fogel, "Emotional and Physical Pain Activate Similar Brain Regions," *Psychology Today*, April 19, 2012, https://www.psychologytoday.com/us/blog/body-sense/201204/emotional-and-physical-pain-activate-similar-brain-regions, accessed February 4, 2021.

162 *The Gayatri Mantra*: Gayatri Mantra: Meaning and Significance," *Times of India*, April 9, 2020, https://timesofindia.indiatimes.com/religion/mantras-chants/meaning

-and-significance-of-the-gayatri-mantra/articleshow/7506
5013.cms, accessed February 4, 2021.

163 *from Durkheim to Freud to Kierkegaard*: Émile Durkheim, *The Elementary Forms of the Religious Life* (New York: Free Press, 1965). Sigmund Freud. *Civilization and Its Discontents* (New York: Norton, 1961). Soren Kierkegaard, *Fear and Trembling and the Sickness unto Death,* trans. Walter Lowrie (Princeton, NJ: Princeton University Press, 2013).

163 *By combining the results*: Jonathan Jong, Robert Ross, Tristan Philip, Si-Hua Chang, Naomi Simons, and Jamin Halberstadt, "The Religious Correlates of Death Anxiety: A Systematic Review and Meta-Analysis," *Religion, Brain and Behavior* 8, no. 1 (2018): 4–20, doi: 10.1080/2153599X.2016.1238844.

165 *even atheists show an uptick*: Ara Norenzayan and Ian G. Hansen, "Belief in Supernatural Agents in the Face of Death," *Personality and Social Psychology Bulletin* 32, no. 2 (2006): 174–87, doi: 10.1177/0146167205280251. Jonathan Jong, Jamin Halberstadt, and Matthias Bluemke,"Foxhole Atheism, Revisited: The Effects of Mortality Salience on Explicit and Implicit Religious Belief," *Journal of Experimental Social Psychology* 48, no. 5 (2012): 983–89, doi: 10.1016/j.jesp.2012.03.005.

166 *Steven Pinker summed up*: Glen T. Stanton, "Steven Pinker and WaPo Are Wrong. Belief in Heaven Isn't a COVID Deathwish," *The Federalist*, May 28, 2020, https://thefederalist.com/2020/05/28/steven-pinker-and-wapo-are-wrong-belief-in-heaven-isnt-a-covid-death-wish/, accessed February 4, 2021.

167 *One finding that's often used*: Daniella M. Kupor, Kristin Laruin, and Jonathan Levav, "Anticipating Divine Protection? Reminders of God Can Increase Nonmoral Risk Taking," *Psychological Science* 26, no. 4 (2015): 374–84, doi: 10.1177/095679 7614563108.

167 *Subsequent studies with more people*: Will M. Gervais, Stephanie E. McKee, and Sarah Malik, "Do Religious Primes Increase Risk Taking? Evidence Against 'Anticipating Divine Protection' in Two Preregistered Direct Replications of Kupor, Laurin, and Levav (2015)," *Psychological Science* 31, no. 7 (2020): 858–64, doi: 10.1177/0956797620922477.

167 *Judaism in particular*: Elliot N. Dorff, *The Jewish Tradition: Religious Beliefs and Healthcare Decisions* (Chicago: Park Ridge Center for the Study of Health, Faith, and Ethics, 1996).

169 *As Rabbi Benjamin Resnick*: Benjamin Resnick, "Aninut: Between Death and Burial," My Jewish Learning, https://www.myjewishlearning.com/article/aninut-between-death-and-burial/, accessed February 4, 2021.

171 *But if you look*: Camille B. Wortman and Roxanne C. Silver, "The Myths of Coping with Loss," *Journal of Consulting and Clinical Psychology* 57, no. 3 (1989): 349–57, doi: 10.1037/0022-006X.57.3.349.

171 *The psychologist George Bonanno*: George A. Bonanno et al., "Resilience to Loss and Chronic Grief: A Prospective Study from Preloss to 18-month Postloss," *Journal of Personality and Social Psychology* 83, no. 5 (2002): 1150–64, doi: 10.1037/0022-3514.83.5.1150.

172 *Demonstrating the power of religion*: Gerhild Becker, Carola J. Xander, Hubert E. Blum, Johannes, Lutterback, Felix Momm, Marjolein Gysels, and Irene J. Higginson, "Do Religious or Spiritual Beliefs Influence Bereavement? A Systematic Review," *Palliative Medicine* 21, no. 3 (2007): 207–17, doi: 10.1177/0269216307077327.

172 *reducing the duration of their grief*: Kiri Walsh, Michael King, Louise Jones, Adrian Tookman, and Robert Blizard, "Spiritual Beliefs May Affect Outcome of Bereavement:

Prospective Study," *BMJ* 324, no. 7353 (2002): 1551, doi: 10.1136/bmj.324.7353.1551.

172 *Three main factors*: Bonanno 1150-1164. George A. Bonanno, Camille B. Wortman, and Randolph M. Nesse," Prospective Patterns of Resilience and Maladjustment During Widowhood," *Psychology and Aging* 19, no. 2 (2004): 260–71, doi: 10 .1037/0882-7974.19.2.260.

173 *So reinforcing positive memories*: Ibid.

173 *As Rabbi Lord Jonathan Sacks*: "How to recite the Mourner's Kaddish," Torah Café, https://www.torahcafe.com/rabbi-lord -jonathan-sacks/how-to-recite-the-mourners-kaddish-video _825a5f3e1.html, accessed February 25, 2021.

175 *looking into a mirror*: Michael F. Scheier and Charles S. 175, "Self-Focused Attention and the Experience of Emotion: Attraction, Repulsion, Elation, and Depression," *Journal of Personality and Social Psychology* 35, no. 9 (1977): 625–36, doi: 10.1037/0022-3514.35.9.625.

175 *Other experiments have found*: Joanne V. Wood, Judith A. Saltzberg, John M. Neale, Arthur A. Stone, and Tracy B. Rachmiel, "Self-Focused Attention, Coping Responses, and Distressed Mood in Everyday Life," *Journal of Personality and Social Psychology* 58, no. 6 (1990): 1027–36, doi: 10.1037/0022 -3514.58.6.1027.

176 *repeated offsets of mild pain*: Joseph C. Franklin, Kent M. Lee, Eleanor K. Hanna, and Mitchell J. Prinstein, "Feeling Worse to Feel Better: Pain-Offset Relief Simultaneously Stimulates Positive Affect and Reduces Negative Affect," *Psychological Science* 24, no. 4 (2012): 521–29, doi: 10.1177/0956797612458805. Cindy Harmon-Jones, Emily Hinton, Judy Tien, Elizabeth Summerell, and Brock Bastian, "Pain Offset Reduces Rumination in Response to Evoked Anger and Sadness," *Journal of*

Personality and Social Psychology 117, no. 6 (2019): 1189–1202, doi: 10.1037/pspp0000240.

178 *The mind interprets giving*: Elizabeth Dunn and Michael Norton, *Happy Money: The Science of Smarter Spending* (New York: Simon & Schuster, 2013).

181 *They have more empathy*: Daniel Lim and David DeSteno, "Suffering and Compassion: The Links Among Adverse Life Experiences, Empathy, Compassion, and Prosocial Behavior," *Emotion* 16, no. 2 (2016): 175–82, doi: 10.1037/emo0000144.

181 *They're even more resistant*: Daniel Lim and David DeSteno, "Past Adversity Protects Against the Numeracy Bias in Compassion," *Emotion* 20, no. 8 (2020): 1344–56, doi: 10.1037/emo0000655.

Epilogue

184 *dropped from 51 percent to 43 percent*: Ian Lovett, "Institutional Religion's Role is Declining in the U.S.," *Wall Street Journal*, December 17, 2019, https://www.wsj.com/articles/institutional-religions-role-is-declining-in-the-u-s-11576633657, accessed February 4, 2021.

184 *As Alison Gopnik noted*: Alison Gopnik, "When Truth and Reason Are No Longer Enough," *Atlantic*, April 2018, https://www.theatlantic.com/magazine/archive/2018/04/steven-pinker-enlightenment-now/554054/, accessed February 4, 2021.

185 *But in the long run*: Martin Nowak and Roger Highfield, *Supercooperators* (New York: Free Press, 2011).

186 *we've also become less happy*: Christopher Ingraham, "Americans Are Becoming Less Happy, and There's Research To

Prove It," *Los Angeles Times*, March 23, 2019, https://www.la
times.com/science/sciencenow/la-sci-sn-americans-less-happy
-20190323-story.html, accessed February 4, 2021.

186 *27 percent of US adults*: Michael Lipka and Claire Gecewicz,
"More Americans Now Say They're Spiritual but Not Religious," Pew Research Center, September 6, 2017, https://
www.pewresearch.org/fact-tank/2017/09/06/more-americans
-now-say-theyre-spiritual-but-not-religious/, accessed February 4, 2021.

186 *two-thirds of people*: Pew Research Center, "Why Americans Go
(and Don't Go) to Religious Services," Pew Forum, August 1,
2018, https://www.pewforum.org/2018/08/01/why-americans
-go-to-religious-services/, accessed February 4, 2021.

188 *a higher percentage of Jews*: Emma Green, "Why Orthodox
Judaism is Appealing to So Many Millennials," *Atlantic*,
March 31, 2016, https://www.theatlantic.com/politics/archive
/2016/03/orthodox-judaism-millennials/476118/, accessed February 4, 2021.

188 *fewer Orthodox Jews*: Alan Cooperman and Gregory A. Smith,
"Eight Facts About Orthodox Jews from the Pew Research
Survey," Pew Research Institute, October 17. 2013, https://
www.pewresearch.org/fact-tank/2013/10/17/eight-facts-about
-orthodox-jews-from-the-pew-research-survey/, accessed February 4, 2021.

188 *The story among Christians*: Michael Lipka, "Mainline Protestants Make Up Shrinking Number of U.S. Adults," Pew Research Institute, https://www.pewresearch.org/fact-tank/2015
/05/18/mainline-protestants-make-up-shrinking-number-of
-u-s-adults/, accessed February 4, 2021. Jonathan M. Pitts, "Con-
versions Gradually Transforming Orthodox Christianity,"
Baltimore Sun, June 24, 2017, https://www.baltimoresun.com

/maryland/bs-md-non-greek-greek-orthodox-priest-2017 0624-story.html, accessed February 4, 2021.

188 *Even the number of young women*: Eve Fairbanks, "Behold, the Millennial Nuns," *HuffPost Highline,* July 11, 2019, https://www.huffpost.com/highline/article/millennial-nuns/, accessed February 4, 2021.

188 *interest in the "old ways"*: "Designing Worship Spaces with Millennials in Mind," Barna, November 5, 2014, https://www .barna.com/research/designing-worship-spaces-with-millen nials-in-mind/#.VFuicvmsVX8, accessed February 4, 2021.

190 *He described WOTF*: Mark Harris, "Inside the First Church of Artificial Intelligence," *Wired*, November 15, 2017, https:// www.wired.com/story/anthony-levandowski-artificial-intel ligence-religion/, accessed February 4, 2021.

190 *a robot named Mindar*: Sigal Samuel, "Robot Priests Can Bless You, Advise You, and Even Perform Your Funeral," Vox, January 13, 2020, https://www.vox.com/future-perfect /2019/9/9/20851753/ai-religion-robot-priest-mindar-buddhism -christianity.

191 *With that explosive growth*: Livia Gershon, "Who Is Santa Muerte?" JSTOR Daily, October 5, 2020, https://daily.jstor .org/who-is-santa-muerte/, accessed February 25, 2021.

192 *Sacred Design Lab*: "How We Work," Sacred Design Lab, https://sacred.design/how-we-work, accessed February 4, 2021.

Index

Index

baby boomers, 121

Banisteriopsis caapi, 104

baptism, 80

bar mitzvah, bat mitzvah, 77–79

becoming, as human need, 193

belief:
  placebo effect and, 127–32
  religious, *see* religious beliefs
  social aspects of, 130–31

Bell, Catherine, 8

belonging, *see* connection

beyond, sense of, 193

birthday celebrations, 27

blue zones, 122

body position, 52–53

Bonanno, George, 171–72, 173

bonding, parent-child, 29–30
  rituals and, 30, 32–35

Bowlby, John, 98

Brahma, mysticism in, 97

brahmacharya, 141

brain:
  altered neural patterns in, 94
  default mode network of, 102–3, 104, 107
  development of, in adolescents, 82
  see also mind

breathing, 91, 92–94, 100

Brooks, David, 143

Bruhn, John, 124

Buddhists, Buddhism, 41, 43, 44, 155, 157, 180, 190
  afterlife as viewed by, 165–66

contemplation of mortality in, 147–48

meditation practices in, 10–11, 110, 134–36, 147–48

mysticism in, 96, 97

science and, 5–6

Buettner, Dan, 122

bullet ants, 65–66

Cabot, Richard Clarke, 128

cancer:
  psilocybin and, 111
  religious practices and, 119
  traditional healing methods and, 12–13

cardiovascular disease, religious practices and, 118, 123–24

caretaking, 25

Carstensen, Laura, 148–49, 157

Catholic Mass:
  modernization of, 187–88
  scientific studies of, 54–55

Catholics, Catholicism, 5, 53, 123–24, 145
  anointing of the sick in, 126, 160–61, 164–65
  confession in, 154, 160, 164–65
  confirmation in, 80–81
  Holy Communion in, 160, 161
  Last Rites in, 160–61, 162, 164–65

certainty, sense of, religious belief and, 16, 17, 120

Changing Woman (*Asdzáá Nádleehé*), 68–69

Index

Index

Index

Index

Index

Index

self-control and, 56–57, 59

mortality, growing sense of, 143–51, 153, 157–58, 195

mortality rate, religious practices and, 117–18

mothers:
bonding of infants with, 29–30
isolation of, 40–41
postpartum depression in, 36–37
as primary caretakers of children, 32, 36
rituals in relieving burdens on, 36

movement:
in ritualized prayer, 51–53
see also synchrony

mysticism, 89
ayahuasca and, 104–6
Buddhist, 96, 97
Christian, 96–97, 99–101
connection with divine as goal of, 95–97
Hindu, 97, 103
magic mushrooms and, 106–8
marriage and, 87–88
religious orders and, 99
scaffolding in, 98, 102, 104, 105–6, 109–11
scientific research on, 100–101, 102–4, 107–8
sense of security in, 98–99
transcendence and, *see* transcendence

namakarana, 27–28

naming rituals, 25–26, 27–29
convergence across religions of, 28

National Social Life, Health, and Aging Project, 122

Native Americans, sweat rituals of, 136–39

neural entertainment, 94

New Medical Dictionary, A (1785), 128

Nietzsche, Friedrich, 183–84

Nine Contemplations of Atisha, 148

Noble Eightfold Path, 43

nudges, ritualized, 54–64

Obama Foundation, 192–93

obiiwai, 25

okuizome, 26–27

omiyamairi, 26, 27

onein, 169

onusa, 26

oshichiya, 25–26, 27

oxytocin, 30

pain:
in coming-of-age rituals, 65–69, 73–77, 79, 82–83
of grief, 159, 169, 171

pain relief, expectation and, 128–29

parents, parenting, 30–31
emotional, physical, and financial costs of, 30–32

Index

Index

Index

Index

Index